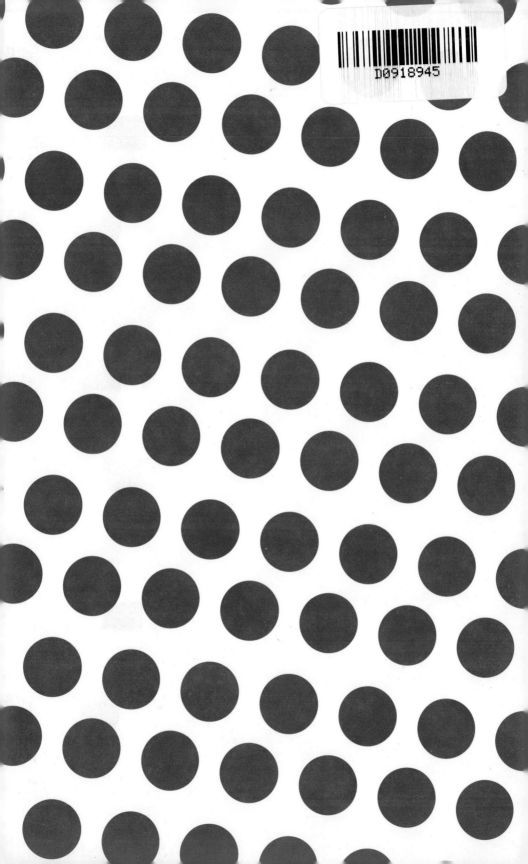

# ENTERTAINING IS FUN!

BOOKS BY

DOROTHY DRAPER

ENTERTAINING IS FUN!

DECORATING IS FUN!

# ENTERTAINING IS FUN!

### HOW TO BE A POPULAR HOSTESS BY DOROTHY DRAPER

WITH LINE CUTS AND HALFTONE ILLUSTRATIONS

*RIZZOLI*

This edition first published in the United States in 2004 by
Rizzoli International Publications, Inc.
300 Park Avenue South
New York, NY 10010
www.rizzoliusa.com

© 1941 by Dorothy Draper
Introduction © 2004 by Carleton Varney
First Rizzoli edition published 2004
First published by Doubleday, Doran & Company, Inc. in 1941.

2004 2005 2006 2007 / 10 9 8 7 6 5 4 3 2 1

Printed in the United States

ISBN: 0-8478-2619-8

Library of Congress Catalog Control Number: 2004108225

To

MAY DAVIE

*a loyal and understanding friend*

*and*

*a gay and delightful hostess*

# INTRODUCTION

Outrageous, controversial, and irreverent, Dorothy Draper was the top decorator of her time—perhaps of all time. The great great granddaughter of one of the signers of the Declaration of Independence, Dorothy Draper was born in 1889, in the exclusive community of Tuxedo Park, New York. Brought up in this elite milieu where beautiful surroundings were a birthright, she broke with tradition by turning her artistic sense into a profitable and groundbreaking career.

Dorothy Draper truly reinvented the profession of interior decorating, and shaped what the profession has become today. She rejected the dowdy color schemes of the Edwardian times, and replaced them with brilliant colors, big floral patterns, bold stripes, and the contrasting colors that became her trademark. It was not uncommon to see a Dorothy Draper–decorated room with aqua-and-white striped walls, vibrant "lipstick red" carpeting, and curtains made of a flowery chintz: pink, violet, and red roses entwined with vibrant green leaves and aqua blue ribbons on a sparkling crisp white background. At a time when creating period stuffy settings was a society lady's goal, Dorothy dismissed the use of the old reliables as insecurity, or remnants of infantile experience and exposure. She ignored what some might call "historical accuracies" in her decorating plans. Her advice was to cheerfully mix periods. She thought nothing about cutting a painting in two, when the single canvas was too large for a specific wall space and when a pair of canvases would work better over the console tables at each side of a drawing room fireplace.

During World War II, when furnishings and decorative products were not readily available, she took to using large, brilliantly colored painted stencils, sometimes of a damask design, for wall decorations. She often created coffee tables by painting antique, round, twenty-nine-inch-high dining tables white, or black with gold trim, and simply chopping off the legs. Then she would frequently hand-paint the coffee-table top with some very handsome striping or pattern—another of her decorative touches. When lamps were unavailable, brass firedogs might be put into use, topped with accordion-pleated shades, entwined with black grosgrain ribbon and tied with bows as an added trim. She would even tell a client to dye her Persian rug, or paint the frames of her eighteenth-century dining room chairs.

Dorothy Draper's interiors formed the backdrop for the elite of her day. When she painted the row houses on Sutton Place black,

black, and black, with white trim and shining colored doors, like the doors of Dublin, she transformed the then-shabby East Side blocks into the chicest, most prestigious of New York neighborhoods. Another one of her coups was the renovation of the Greenbrier Hotel at White Sulphur Springs, West Virginia, for which it has been reported that she received, at the time, the largest fee ever paid to a decorator for her talents. At the opening of the hotel in 1948, Dorothy was one of the star attractions along with others, including the Duke and Duchess of Windsor, the Astors, the Vanderbilts, and the Whitneys. The Greenbrier, to this day, has remained a larger-than-life resort hotel—true to the Dorothy Draper tradition.

Included among the many properties that became landmarks of the Draper touch were New York's Hampshire House, San Francisco's Fairmont and Mark Hopkins hotels, Arrowhead Springs Hotel at Lake Arrowhead, California, the Dining "Pool Room" of New York's Metropolitan Museum of Art, the Quitandinha in Petropólis, Brazil, and the Camilia House at the Drake Hotel in Chicago. Dorothy Draper's designs carried right into the age of air travel when she planned the interiors for the Convair 880 airplane for the General Dynamics Corporation. From hotels to hospitals, automobile interiors, and supermarkets, Dorothy Draper left her mark on the American landscape.

When it came to entertaining and decorating, Dorothy thought about the tabletop as she thought about a room. The tablecloth was to be treated as a wall. The color or design had to be perfect: bright azalea, polka dots, or green and white awning stripes. The tabletop was the background for the china patterns. China patterns were designs just as curtains and the flatware and crystal were accessories like lamps and pillows. They had to be coordinated and perfect.

Through her writing in *Good Housekeeping* and through her nationally syndicated newspaper column, "Ask Dorothy Draper," her influence—which has carried into our times and will most likely carry into the future—has spread far beyond her original base. Her style is widely imitated.

I arrived at Dorothy Draper & Company in the very early Sixties, a young Oberlin College graduate. I became an assistant to the then-president of the company, Leon Hegwood. Mrs. Draper was chairman of the company's board. I vividly recall Mrs. Draper's appearance: Tall and imposing, head topped with a bright strawberry satin hat, full black cape, gloves, and penetrating eyes. She reminded me of a female Roman gladiator, ready to conquer all she viewed—and definitely ready to decorate or redecorate all she viewed. On a train ride with her to Philadelphia one day, early in my career, she told me that there was no such thing as good taste or bad taste, there was only taste; and that every person or property had his or her own character, which should be respected. Dorothy Draper never expressed criticism of the styles created by others. She was always open to new ideas and new discoveries: "If it looks right, it is right," she would say. (Though what she meant was if it looked right to *her*, it was right.)

And so Dorothy stuck to her own style as does the company, Dorothy Draper & Company Inc., of which I am president today. To the decorators and entertainers of today and tomorrow, who aspire to follow in the Draper tradition, welcome to the wonderful world of color. In honor of Dorothy's individualistic spirit, the royalties from the sale of this reissue of *Entertaining Is Fun* (originally penned by Draper in 1941) will benefit the Dorothy Draper Scholarship Fund. Established at the University of Charleston, West Virginia, in the shadows of Dorothy's beloved Greenbrier Hotel, this fund ensures that her legacy of taste, talent, and courage will endure for years to come. I think she would have wanted it that way.

# PREFACE

## BY ELOISE DAVISON

For anyone who has not allowed herself to become discouraged with the years entertaining one's friends is a vital part of living. But entertaining must be fun. It must be fun for the guests and, what is just as important, fun for the hostess herself.

Anyone who has been to Dorothy Draper's parties or to a party where she was a guest knows how truly she believes this! A party must be fun to plan, fun to give, fun to go to. Unless it is, it isn't a party, it's an obligation or a sacrificed evening.

Only someone like Dorothy Draper, enriched by years of brilliant living and surrounded by interesting friends, could have written this stimulating, useful book, *Entertaining Is Fun*. The background for it has required living on a charming, scintillating level, surrounded by friends who have been worth the effort required to make life fun for them as well as for herself. That kind of living doesn't just happen. There are basic rules to know and understand, and Dorothy Draper gives them here.

Her formulae given for successful parties are built of helpful, concise, practical tips on entertaining gaily. A novice will find specific help on turning to this book. A timid person who hesitates to invite important people will find courage here. A seasoned hostess can get a revitalizing spark that will help her with her next party providing—and Dorothy Draper is stern about this—she wants her party to be an amusing one.

One will think twice, after reading this book, before blaming any party that fails on uninteresting guests. Dorothy Draper believes that it's up to the hostess, once she's invited guests to her home, to find that smoldering spark of interest that nine times out of ten can be fanned into an active flame providing you know how to go about it. She tells you how to do it. She's decidedly outspoken about the heckled hostess who hovers in a frenzy over too-elaborate food until she has the air infested with her anguish, or the one who ambitiously assembles as guests a galaxy of stars so bright they cancel out each other in the struggle to outshine but leave a party flat and uninspired.

Give a conventional formal party if you must, but remember that a simple unpretentious one is just as much a party, providing either type is planned to the last detail, including those distinctive gay touches that make your party peculiarly your own, and executed with that careful carelessness that keeps the hostess in control without dictating.

From that infectious sparkle with which the hostess must meet the first guest until the last reluctant person leaves any hostess must be at her happy best. Any party can fall pitifully flat no matter how much or how little is spent, how good or how poor the food or how well or poorly chosen the guests, unless the hostess keeps in gala mood. The guiding rules are here to help you to invite, to plan, to set the stage, to create that *gala* feeling.

Only these people should read this book: those who like to give a gay party; those who like a pleasant evening with friends; those who dread to give a party; those who fear a party; those who have been bored at a party; those who have gone to a party that went flat—or, worse still, given one; those who do not have unlimited money to spend on entertaining. On second thought I'd add one more group: those who don't like a party. It will serve them right to find out why. Here's a tip— in Dorothy Draper's world there is no room for martyrs with a "determined will to be dreary."

This book is most timely. If you've let this grim, chaotic world befog, upset or make you melancholy and indifferent about entertaining, *Entertaining Is Fun* should be your meat. There's every chance it will jog you out of the doldrums and make you remember that living is more vital when you share some hospitality with your friends.

# CONTENTS

CONTENTS

# 1

# YOU DON'T NEED

## Prepare to Lose Some Old Ideas

THIS IS A BOOK on *making living fun*. On having your friends to the house, and on how to give them a good time. And, incidentally, on how to give yourself a very good time as well.

This is also a book on how to deal firmly with your Will to Be Dreary. (Of course if you insist upon being resigned to life and terribly serious about it this is *not* the book for you.) This is a book on how to face the changing conditions of life gaily and how to develop your life to include new friends, new interests, fresh and exciting ideas.

Have you ever considered how much ridiculous pomposity surrounds the word "entertaining"? And the idea which has been built up that you *must* do this and you *must* do that? This is a book which (we hope) will explode those old ideas. We hope it will banish forever the idea that you have to have a lot of money to have a good time yourself and to give other people good times too.

## Where It All Begins

So LET'S START with your front door, which fulfills two purposes. It swings open to let you out into the world and to all sorts of thrilling adventures there. But also that same door opens in to permit the outside world (or as much of it as *you* choose) to come in, bringing friends, laughter, good times and the stimulus of new, inspiring ideas.

You don't need to go outside your door for any of these things. You don't need to scan the theater and restaurant advertisements in the evening papers in search of amusement. All that you have to do is to open your front door (and incidentally your heart). A great deal of fun can come in that friendly, open door. Fun is something all of us need, perhaps never more so than just now. And to have fun, or happiness if you like the word better, is very important in life—is the one fundamental—and only real reason for entertaining at all.

Right here and now let me say that I wish there was a word to replace that rather stilted one "entertaining." The word sounds pompous and effortful. I have searched the dictionary for a substitute which will express more closely what I mean by the longer and rather cumbersome phrase which, nevertheless, I like better, "having your friends to the house."

But the dictionaries have failed me. We shall have to go on talking about entertaining. Only please remember this: when I use it I mean nothing fussy or strained. Nothing done for effect. By "entertaining" I mean having a good time with your friends in your own home and giving them a good time, too. But done with a flair.

"But," you may say, "the etiquette books don't make it sound as simple as that." Of course they don't. They go into a dither over salad forks and engraved invitations. They try to make you believe that being a hostess means parking your natural, friendly, everyday self and putting on a personality for the occasion that is as stiff and uncomfortable as your great-grandmother's hoop skirt. And as old-fashioned.

Today fussy, formal parties are definitely out of style. Smart people won't be bothered with that sort of thing. They want to enjoy themselves, to have fun. And they want to have a hostess who isn't worrying so hard over her party that she can't have a good time with her friends. If you want to be a shining success as a hostess begin right now by starting off on a new tack. Stop thinking about what is or isn't correct. Instead, think about *you* yourself.

A *delighted* hostess is a *delightful* hostess. Plan your party so that you and your husband (we hope you have one) will have a good time and your guests will have the time of their lives. They'll tell you so, and with an enthusiasm which goes right down to their toes. You can believe them because all that they say will be true.

A little while ago I wrote a book about how to have fun decorating your house. Decorating and entertaining are halves of the same apple. They are important parts of the art of living. The psychologists cite dozens of case histories of people who are ill because they are living lonely, uninteresting lives in drab or uninspiring surroundings. There are many people who, whether they know it or not, are wilting away for want of some fun and a social life. *A lovely place to live, congenial companionship and real fun and amusement are human needs.* They are as important as sunlight and fresh air. You can't be healthy and you can't be successful without them. I really mean this.

If you are one of those who hold back from asking your friends to the house because entertaining seems so difficult, the first thing is to get rid of all the bugaboos the etiquette books have set up for you to be afraid of. No matter what any of them may say, to entertain successfully

## YOU DON'T NEED

1. A lot of money.
2. A big house.
3. A staff of well-trained servants.
4. Expensive, elaborate food.
5. Professional entertainers.
6. A luxurious setting.

Of course if you are among the fortunate but very few who don't have to worry about a budget and keeping within it then it's likely that any number of delightful, original ideas (though I've known rich people who had boring parties) for giving your friends a good time will occur to you without any trouble at all. Who, for instance, hasn't thought it would be thrilling to rent a private car and take a party of friends interested in racing to the Kentucky Derby? Or, if you happened to have a big country house, that it would be amusing to fill it with lights, hothouse flowers and expensive decorations, to set the terraces with smart new furniture, gay cushions and lots of potted plants; to put up half a dozen tropical-colored cabanas on the beach—if there *is* a beach—and to ask a houseful of interesting, good-looking people down for the week end?

There's no trick at all to *that*.

The trick, and there is one, of course, and more than just one, is to entertain successfully and delightfully without all or even any of these props. "Impossible," you say. Not a bit of it. It can be done. It takes courage, of course. And originality. It calls for intelligent planning in advance. It demands that you have something within you that might be called a *flair for enjoyment.*

## Wills and Won'ts

IN RECENT YEARS we have all heard a good deal about the Will to Fail, which sometimes is even more urgent than the Will to Succeed. The Will to Fail isn't the only enemy most of us have to guard against. There is also the Will to Be Dreary. It's a morose little imp which whispers to us that something which we know would be fun would be too much trouble, will take too much time, is too expensive and probably wouldn't be as amusing after all as just now you think it would be.

Now don't listen to that voice. Tune it out. Don't let it persuade you that because you are married or over forty or because your husband has business worries that you can't have *fun.* There was a woman who never asked her friends to come in to tea simply because she hadn't a silver tea set. At least that is the conscious reason she gave her husband and herself. Actually it wasn't the lack of a silver tea set that prevented her having a normal social life. It was the Will to Be Dreary. That perverse spirit simply seized on the tea set as an excuse. It has a subtle way of doing that. It can provide you with a dozen alibis, all of which sound quite plausible. But don't accept them. Remember what I said a little while ago about fun being good for you. Try the prescription and see how it works.

All my life I have enjoyed having my friends to the house, whether this was a house in town, or a shabby old Admiral's House in Newport, hanging over the harbor, or a tiny two-room New York City apartment. I've always had a good time at my own parties. I think that is what every woman who gives a party should have. The day has gone by, thank goodness, when the hostess made a martyr of herself by taking the dullest, least responsive man among her guests for her dinner partner. Nowadays she picks out the most attractive and interesting men in the room and makes her end of the table the center of the fun.

This isn't selfishness. It's good hostessship. Your enjoyment is as contagious to your guests as the measles. Remember that and dispose of that Victorian martyr complex along with the etiquette books.

Now that we have cleared away all the bugaboos (once and for all, I hope) suppose we consider some of the things you *do* have to have to make a party go.

## YOU DO NEED

1. A hostess who expects to have a good time.
2. Some clever touches which give your home a party feeling.
3. Friendly guests who come prepared to enjoy themselves.
4. Plenty of delicious food, attractively presented.
5. Some element of unexpectedness.

If you will think this list over you will see at once that none of the things I have mentioned are impossible to anyone, living anywhere. They are as readily available if you live in the suburb of a large city, in a town of three thousand on the Nebraska prairie or in a one-room apartment in New York. What is more, none of them depend on anyone but you, yourself. It isn't your husband's fault or your best beau's or your mother's if your last party wasn't the success you'd hoped it would be. It was yours. Somewhere along the line you slipped up. But don't feel too badly about it. Read over again the list I have just given you and diagnose your own trouble. The next thing is to consider how to set it right.

All of the MUSTS on the list start not with what you *have* but with what *you are*. That's the really important thing about them. Every party revolves around its hostess. And the success of every party begins with, and depends on, the hostess's feeling about herself.

If you feel that the evening is going to be fun your husband is bound to catch this feeling from you. There are men who have a real gift for entertaining. If you're married to one of them then you have the greatest asset any hostess can possibly have. But also there are shy men and men who would like to entertain and to have their wives ask friends to the house more than they do and who hold off because entertaining seems to present more difficulties than they care to attempt. It's fatally easy—and fatal—for a bachelor to get into the way of going to other people's parties and not giving any of his own. If he persists in the habit long enough he gets the reputation of "always a guest, never a host." He might even be something supplied by a caterer. That's a bad-enough fate, goodness knows. But what makes it worse is that he never finds out how much fun a person can have giving a party all by himself.

Fundamentally there's no real difference between being a successful hostess and being a success as a host. Both start with:

## You, Yourself

YOUR PARTY begins with *you*. We have said that before, but one can't say it too often. How much fun your guests get out of it and how much fun you get out of it depend on how much you know about yourself and what you, yourself, are really like.

So, before you take up pencil and paper and start making plans for your next party, give a little time to getting acquainted with yourself.

All of us exist on two levels. There is the outer YOU, and there is the inner YOU—all that your mirror, your hairdresser, your family and the friends who know you so well that they don't mince matters can tell you. If you're a beauty you are probably fully aware of the fact. There are no unconscious Helen of Troys. And if you're not in the glamour-girl class but still worth considering, well, you know that too.

But how much do you know about the inner YOU? This is the YOU that feels things. If that YOU is shy, sensitive and easily hurt, if it finds it hard to make friends with other people and has to be pushed to do so, then the answer is that probably you have never taken the pains and the time to make friends with yourself. If you will do that you will find at once that other people will flock to you.

Just as all of us suffer at times from that insidious Will to Be Dreary (and even the most adjusted have lapses at times), many of us, through not being well acquainted with ourselves, don't really know what we like or what will make us happy. We go on doing certain things because that is the way we were brought up to do them, or that is how other people we know do them. And we tell ourselves we like them that way. Yet all the time we don't like them that way at all.

No one can possibly give her guests a good time at the sort of party which does not come naturally to her. If you really and truly like parties that are dignified, formal, perfect in every detail—then, by all means, plan to give that sort of party, even if you have only two or three a year. On the other hand, if you happen to be the sort of person who takes fright at this sort of entertaining, or if you find it dull and boring, or if you simply can't afford to entertain formally, then do realize that *nobody today needs to be formal unless she wants to be.* You can entertain at dinner at a card table drawn up before the fire or beside the window with the view. The dinner can be three courses, a soup, a hot dish and a salad with crackers and cheese and coffee. And if the table is charmingly and daintily set, if the food is delicious (and I don't mean expensive), plentiful and served attractively, if you are at your happy best, then it is a party.

There's only one worth-while rule that I know of as regards entertaining: *suit your parties to yourself* and *they will suit your guests.*

How can you be that happy, easy, free, unself-conscious hostess? Your setting has a lot to do with that. It is as important to you as the setting against which the star plays her role. It is not only that your guests *see* you against and in that setting; it is how you *feel* in it yourself.

## Setting the Stage

EVERY GOOD HOSTESS has a sense of showmanship. Some of this has to be hers by native gift; but, cheer up, a lot of it can be acquired.

The good showman knows how to marshal all the forces at his command. He knows how to turn liabilities into assets. He knows values and effects. There's no denying the fact that to come into a room in which there are candles lighted and glowing softly, where a fire crackles on the hearth, where there are flowers, much clear, lovely color in curtains and slip covers, where there is the sound of the cocktails being shaken up against a low undercurrent of music, where there is a hostess in her prettiest, most becoming dress coming to welcome you, gives anyone the sense that the curtain is going up on a delightful and exciting evening.

It's the art of creating that "gala" feeling that makes your success as a hostess, whether the party is for four or for forty. Later on I shall take up in detail some of the things you can do to your house to give it a party feeling. Just now it's enough to call attention to the fact that all this is important to the success of *any* party. Much more important, I believe, than the food you plan to give your guests. Even the most elaborate canapés or drinks or elaborate and delicious dishes won't make up for a sag at the start of the evening. At any party the first fifteen minutes are the most important quarter hour during the whole time the party lasts. Get your party off to a good start, and after that it will go of itself.

## Your Guests

PRESUMABLY THESE PEOPLE you are expecting are not strange animals out of the zoo. They are your friends. They are May and Preston, Marjorie and Fair and Gladys and Henry. Even if you have added two or three other people you don't know as well, who may have entertained you and your husband and to whom you feel under an obligation, there's nothing devastating they can do to the evening.

All of us sigh at times for some new, interesting people to invite. All the interesting people don't live in the cities. Or even in two or three cities. That idea is one of the alibis we give ourselves for not going adventuring in whatever locality we happen to live in. A woman I know who lives in a small New England village thought that. Then she discovered by chance a trailer parked in a wood lot three miles out from town and, living in it, a couple who looked decidedly interesting. The man turned out to be a foreign correspondent for a big newspaper, who was combining a vacation out of doors with the writing of an important book. The wife was an illustrator. My friend asked them to dinner and asked two or three other couples to meet them. It was a most successful evening, chiefly, I believe, because it gave the hostess and several of her friends the assurance that new and interesting things could happen even in that little village in the Litchfield hills.

Another alibi is the idea that of course *you* couldn't ask the famous Mr Wintergreen who has just come back from exploring the jungles of Costa Rica to dinner. You have met Mr Wintergreen. In fact, you had a delightful conversation with him after the lecture he gave your club. But somehow the fact that he has been written up so much in the newspapers seems to put him beyond your reach.

Nonsense. It's ten to one that Mr Wintergreen would adore to be asked to dinner and to tell you and several of your friends about his adventures. You may take it for granted that most people, even the ones the world considers the most successful, feel lonely and insecure inside themselves at times. And for that lonely, insecure feeling there's nothing so helpful as to be invited and welcomed and made much of, even in a very simple, informal way.

The dullest parties in the world are the ones that are made up entirely of "interesting people." The best parties are the ones at which friends are brought together to enjoy themselves. So relax. When you hear the first ring of the doorbell *smile*. Remember, all this is for fun.

## What Makes a Party Go?

Now THAT WE'VE CONSIDERED the hostess's attitude toward herself and her guests, and her setting which, I insist, is the rock on which all successful entertaining rests, let's think for a moment about the food. Food has been a symbol of hospitality for so many ages that it's all nonsense for the diet faddists to try to scare us out of the idea of offering a guest something to eat. In fact, everyone knows there is something very heart-warming about being offered a glass of sherry or a cocktail or tea or a glass of fruit juice immediately on coming into a house.

And I repeat, *immediately*. Is there anything more ghastly than standing about, waiting for guests to gather and for a party to begin? A drink of some sort or other helps even the shyest person over that awkward moment.

Everyone has his own taste in foods. But there are certain rules that hold good over very simple as well as elaborate dishes and menus. Hot foods should be *very, very hot*. Cold foods and drinks should be *very, very cold*. One really superlative dish is better than two or three mediocre ones. But always, whatever you have, there *should be lots of it*.

The best food in the world is all the better—and foods less good are considerably helped—by being served attractively and in interesting containers. These need not be handsome or expensive. Salad is never more appetizing than when served in a large wooden bowl. And think of the delightful effect of crisp red radishes mixed with lettuce and water cress when so arranged. Or a ring of tomato jelly, thoroughly chilled and filled with string beans marinated in French dressing. Or a red casserole filled with well-browned spaghetti. Or homely, but delectable, black-bean soup served in yellow or orange bowls. Black-bean soup cries out for a slice of lemon atop, for looks as much as for the flavor.

Remember, lovely color plays a lot of tricks with our appetites. If you are serving a white meat, like creamed chicken, for instance, don't add the pallid effect of mashed potato, plain boiled rice, creamed celery, onion or cauliflower. Instead, think of a color scheme. If you have a white meat and one white vegetable, such as boiled rice, then serve a green vegetable, peas or string beans. Add the piquant color as well as the flavor of cranberry sauce or currant jelly. And do give the creamed chicken a sprinkle of paprika.

Use color intelligently in your table settings too. But don't be afraid to use it.

Today the trend everywhere is toward simpler entertaining. This means simpler foods. Some of the whipped cream is going out of American life (fortunately for our figures). Americans generally have discovered the appetizing qualities of some of the dishes which are part of the daily fare of European peoples—Hungarian goulash, *risotto*, spaghetti and chicken livers, French onion soup served in a big ruddy-brown casserole, with toasted bread and freshly grated Parmesan cheese. Too, they are rediscovering how good many of our native American dishes are—Boston baked beans, clam chowder, buckwheat cakes and well-browned country sausage, hot corn breads, fish cakes and, of course, corned-beef hash with a poached egg atop each portion. (As I read this over it sounds tempting but fattening.)

The surprise element you add to your party may be in the way of an exciting new dish which you believe none of your guests have ever met before. One woman I know makes it a rule to serve something new at every party she gives. She says it makes the party more exciting for her, which is the best reason in the world for doing this. Other women feel that they can be more confident and feel freer to enjoy their guests if the menu is one they have tried out many times before.

It's all a matter of personal preference.

Or your surprise element may be some new and interesting person, like Mr Wintergreen, whom you have screwed up the courage to invite after all. Or it may be a thrilling idea or a new story, which you hold back like the ace of trumps, to play at the strategic moment.

A clever hostess always has something up her sleeve. She may not use it. If she is really clever she will not have to. But she knows that she holds something which can start things going if the party hits a snag. This gives her confidence and poise.

But deliver us from the hostess-dictator who marches you from the table just when the conversation has ripened promisingly in order to have coffee in the chilly drawing room. And when the ice has thawed there and the party feeling has started again, arbitrarily orders you off to play games, or see the movies she took on her last trip to Mexico, or to listen to her pet radio program, willy-nilly, whether you want to or not.

No one enjoys an evening which has been worked out on paper in advance. But here again I come back to my premise: the hostess must always be in control. Though her intent and her privilege are to enjoy her own party, she must be constantly aware of her guests and whether each and every one of them is having a good time. *One person who is left out can spoil a whole party.*

The test of every pudding is in the eating. You know—and no one better—whether your party was a success. If you will think it over afterward, and as you think over other people's parties and analyze what made them amusing and delightful or dull, you will learn wherein lies the secret of successful entertaining. That is why I feel you will be interested in some of the little stories which you will find at the end of my chapters.

## CASE HISTORY OF A LADY WHO GAVE HERSELF A PARTY INSTEAD OF A PILL

The Summerwells didn't make any bones about it. They said quite frankly that the reason they gave up their big apartment in town, put most of the furniture in storage and moved to a small house in a suburb so small it took the railroad one hour and seventeen minutes to find it was to save money.

The friends they left in town who had found George and Dolly's parties such fun lamented first, then shrugged their shoulders. "Let us know when you decide to come back to town," they said.

Dolly was a good sport about it. She adored George. Privately she considered him not only the cleverest, most attractive, best-looking man in Wall Street but in the whole world. She was determined to show him she could help, not be a drag. George was going to find out he had married a woman who could economize.

For three or four months she was so busy with the engrossing occupation of making one dollar do the work of three she had no time to feel lonely.

They didn't know anybody in the suburb they moved to, but Dolly didn't care. One or two women called on her and she returned their calls. She was asked to a women's lunch and to join a bridge club, but she refused both invitations. She said to herself if you accepted invitations you had to return them, and she knew from her and George's experiences in town that entertaining cost money.

What Dolly didn't know was that something in her which had been gay and crisp and charming was fading. Her mouth, which used to quirk up delightfully at the corners, developed a little droop. George didn't know what it was he missed, but he knew he missed something. Dolly knew, and was horrified to find it out, that when George came home at night she couldn't think of a thing to tell him except that the hot-water faucet leaked and that carrots were cheaper.

One morning at breakfast, quite unaccountably, she burst into tears. George was scared out of his wits. "You're nervous as a cat. You haven't been looking well for weeks. You're not yourself. You need to see a doctor. . . ." Then he had to run for the train.

"He didn't even kiss me." Dolly sobbed. Yes, she was badly off as *that*.

After a good cry she began to think over what George had said about a doctor. Nerve specialists were expensive indulgences. She simply could not afford to be as sick as all *that*. "Suppose," she said to herself tentatively, "I didn't have to think of expense at all and I felt the way I do; what would I do?"

She could answer her question at once; I'd ask some friends to the house. I'd give a party.

Lying there on her bed, she planned it. There was that attractive Mrs C—— she had met and thought she would like to know better. She would ask her and two of the women who had called when she and George first moved into the suburb. And for a bit of unexpectedness there was her old friend Rita who had said once she would like to come out for the day. Rita had recently come back from a trip to Alaska and with a new and interesting beau.

The beau gave Dolly her next idea. Afternoon parties in town were fun because frequently there were men at them as well as women. After-

noon parties in the suburbs were usually entirely feminine. She would
make hers an innovation. Rita should be asked to bring her beau; George
would be encouraged to come home on an early train, and she would
scour the countryside for two or three other men who might be available.

Next for the food part of the party. With no maid to help, Dolly decided to feature dramatic simplicity. It should be an English tea, with
really superlative tea and double-thickness cream and some Jamaica rum
for those who preferred the extra flourish of a teaspoonful in a cup. She
would have very thin slices of Pepperidge Farm bread, buttered; a covered dish of hot, toasted and buttered English muffins; a plate of strips of
bacon, broiled dry and kept hot on a piece of brown paper in the oven
until needed, which could be eaten from the fingers; globs of apricot jam
to be spread on the hot muffins. And a little turquoise-colored pot of
Persian honey, as decorative as its contents were delicious.

When the hour for the party arrived Dolly surveyed her preparations
with satisfaction. She did not regret her silver tea set, which was stored at
the bank, because the brass kettle shone so brightly and purred so cozily.
The flowered china tea set was charming and repeated the color in the
pots of flowering spring bulbs on the window sills. The tea table itself
was low and generously large. Dolly had stood over George while he
sawed six inches off its legs only the day before.

("Suppose it did belong to your grandmother. She would have cut
down its legs today too.")

She had no tea cloth large enough to cover it, but she had cut one of
her old damask tablecloths in half, hemmed it and then Tintexed this and
a dozen napkins a lovely sky blue. They provided just the right contrast

for the yellow china and the honey pot. There was also a small wicker basket, lined with big glossy green leaves and piled with luscious, out-of-season strawberries (her one extravagance). A walk into the country the day before had resulted in branches of laurel and hemlock which she placed around the room in big vases.

Nor had she forgotten herself. A big pale pink organdy Toby ruff (which she had seen advertised in *Vogue* and sent for by mail) set off her old basic black dress and gave her a springy look and feeling.

Then there were the guests—Rita and her beau, Mrs C—— and the other woman, the young lawyer from a neighboring town who was running for member of assembly and had called to get their votes, another man whom George had met on the commuter's train and liked and an artist whom Dolly had discovered on one of her country rambles, painting the winter snow scene.

"I don't know what that doctor gave you," George said that evening, "but it certainly has done you good."

The Summerwells' afternoon teas have become quite a feature of life in that particular suburb. They never ask more than eight or ten people at a time. Just enough to seat themselves comfortably around the big tea table (which George now thinks was a great idea to have cut down). The only drink they serve is tea. The food is invariably bread and butter (plenty of it), hot toasted muffins and the crisp bacon which the men love to eat, walking about the room.

But people seem to have more fun there than at some of the more elaborate parties. George no longer talks of "when we move back to town." And Dolly has her eye on a lot and secretly makes pencil sketches of house plans.

The Summerwells have put out roots.

# 2

# MAKING YOUR HOUSE SAY WELCOME

## And Not in a Whisper

EVERY WOMAN KNOWS that it's comparatively easy to meet the world with a smile if you're well dressed. It's wonderful knowing your clothes are smartly cut, well fitted and becoming, even though last year's, and it is amazing what it does to your self-confidence.

Just so the knowledge that the front of your house makes passers-by say to themselves: "I wish I knew the people who live there," and that whenever guests come into your living room they pause involuntarily to exclaim: "How lovely!" encourages even the shyest one of us to see herself in the role of a popular, successful hostess.

From that point on it's only a step to being one.

There's nothing so important as first impressions. They leave an indelible mark which nothing that happens later ever quite wipes out. The stage director knows this and tries to arrange a setting for the first act that will bring an exclamation of delight from the audience the minute the curtain goes up. If he has done that he has captured their attention. He has welded all the diverse and separate individuals in the theater seats into a whole—into an audience.

We have said that the successful hostess always has a gift for showmanship. She knows that to make her party go her guests must put off the shadow of their everyday lives which most of us carry about with us, the worries, the regrets, the little irritations and "leftover states of mind," as one of my friends calls them. Their attention must be caught and brought to a point. To enjoy themselves completely they must be unified, as a theater audience is, for the enjoyment of the play.

How can you do this?

First of all, by making your house extend a welcome to everyone who comes into it. And on every occasion. Just now we are talking about the times when guests are coming, but the same things apply to the days when you are not entertaining and when no guest is expected.

Haven't you often played a game with yourself, looking at houses you passed somewhere and wondering what the people who lived in them were like? I am going to suggest that you try the experiment of looking at your own house from this objective point of view. Don't take anything you see for granted. It's ten chances to one that you'll catch yourself exclaiming: "Good gracious, I never knew the front door needs painting again. The grass doesn't grow well close to the porch. A pair of evergreen trees in white painted wooden tubs—no, I'll ask John to give me a pair of specially designed huge pots for a birthday present—would do wonders. . . ."

Don't leave it at that. Ask for a big brass knocker. Get the tubs or the pots and the trees. A quart of good enamel paint doesn't cost much, and it doesn't require a skilled painter to paint a front door. If you wear rubber gloves and do the work on a sunshiny day when it's fun to putter about outdoors you'll enjoy painting it yourself. And maybe your zeal, and the paint, will extend to the steps too.

There's nothing in the American Constitution to the effect that all front doors have to be white or dark green. Have you ever considered the possible charm of a turquoise-blue door in a pale gray stucco house, with boxes of frilly pink petunias under the front windows and a pair of dwarf apple trees beside the steps? Or a glowing Chinese yellow door, like one of Van Gogh's sunflowers, in a dark timbered house? Think of the mystery that would seem to lie behind the door of a white house that was painted the color of blue gentians in the sun.

Even doors in an apartment house can be painted a lovely singing color that makes your front door different from the others on that floor. Your friends will go to it instinctively the minute they step out of the elevator. A lipstick-red door, white trim, with a brass knocker and pots of English ivy beside it against the impassive white wall turn an apartment into a house at no increase in rent. If the hall is too dark for the ivy to grow there, there are all sorts of cleverly made artificial plants and little trees, used for stage decorations and window displays, that can be bought quite cheaply. You can vary your decorations with the seasons—evergreens in winter, in spring a pair of blossoming dwarf fruit trees.

Nothing adds so much to the beauty and happiness of this world as color. Most of us don't get enough of it into our houses or into our lives. We need it about us every day we live, almost as much as we need sunshine and fresh air and water and food. Without it we droop. Whether we know it or have to go to a psychiatrist to be told so, we suffer a depletion of energy in drab, colorless surroundings (the old Will to Be Dreary). Now promise me that you won't read any more until you paint your door, and get *started*.

Your home's welcome begins right at the front door. If you can make that welcome cheery and friendly simply through the use of a quart of paint and a few hours with the paintbrush, why not do it?

While you're considering the outside of your house have a thought for the front windows. They are like a person's eyes. They look out, but also they tell a great deal about what is going on within. Fresh curtains are a *must*. It's ungenerous (or, at any rate, thoughtless) to take account only of how your curtains look from inside the room. Are they so pretty and interesting, when viewed from outside, that they have a come-hither look? Since most of us do much of our entertaining after dark it is well to examine your house from the outside some evening when the lights are lit. Go into the matter of Venetian blinds; colored, or patterned chintz lining to your curtains perhaps, clean *white* ( not cream) opaque window shades, with the fixed idea of making the first impression of your house count for something to everyone who approaches it.

There's no need to have expensive or showy curtains. Or heavy, stuffy ones either. There's nothing lovelier than crisp white muslin curtains, crossed over the upper sash and looped back to show a pot of blossoming primroses or a perky cyclamen on the window sill (very easy to have a carpenter widen the shelf). Windows so dressed smile beside a well-painted front door with a big shining brass knocker.

If you haven't a knocker on your front door then give yourself the fun of rummaging through the antique shops or the hardware stores until you find one that seems to belong to you. It may be an American spread eagle or a classic urn design. It may be like one some friends of mine brought back from a South American cruise—a lady's hand in brass, with a ring on one finger and a snake bracelet about the wrist, holding a ball which knocks against a countersunk brass plate. Whatever the design you select, it is important that it shall have a relation to the paneling of the door. And be sure it is *big enough to be smart.*

## QUIZ FOR HOUSEHOLDERS

1. Is the front door freshly painted? No alibis now. Paint is cheap, and there is that idle, lonely afternoon you have been dreading. Get busy and surprise your husband and the neighbors. And how about the lighting outside the house and in the garden?

2. Is the knocker polished? Brass should be bright and gleaming. It should *not* be lacquered. There's a sentimental value about lifting a knocker that has been rubbed bright by hand labor.

3. Are there pots of greens or flowering plants on either side of the door?

4. Open the door. Is there a powerful electric-light bulb in the hall? Most halls are too dark. You have a let-down feeling when you step into them. See that your hall is brightly lighted.

5. Have you a big vase of greens, laurel, rhododendron, huckleberry or hemlock during the Christmas season on the console or table in the hall? Or bulbs or some flowering plants?

6. Who opens the front door? If you have a maid to do this does she smile when she responds to the guest's knock or ring at the bell? Does she convey the idea that they are expected and welcome? Or that your having six people to dinner on the evening she planned to go to see a movie has precipitated a domestic crisis? If you are in the habit of opening the front door yourself how good are you at registering hospitality, eagerness and delight? Be severe with yourself on this point. It's so extremely important.

7. Has your hall a good coat closet where there is room and hangers for the guests' wraps? A closet jammed with your own raincoats and umbrellas and the children's sleds and skis doesn't count. If you have no adequate closet have you one of those convenient folding coat racks that can be set up in the hall when you are giving a party and folded away at other times?

8. Have you provided a place in the hall where the guests can have a last-minute prink before a mirror before coming into the living room?

No alibis—get started *now!*

## Finally, the Living Room

AFTER ALL, this is where the party really happens. All that has gone before is a prologue. Important and necessary to the success of the play, but not the drama itself.

This begins when your guests reach the living room. There they should get the glamour feeling of the tall white candles in silver or glass candlesticks that have been lighted before the arrival of the first guest; the open fire blazing cheerily on the hearth, the flowers, the bowls of evergreens, the pots of growing bulbs and blossoming plants, the fresh, lovely colors of curtains and cushions and furniture coverings, the little intimate litter of living—the bag of knitting or needlework, the tapestry frame, the card table with the jigsaw puzzle half done or the backgammon board with its colored counters—the white fox terrier wagging a cordial greeting, the bowl of goldfish, or the canary or the finches in their cages; the little table with the decanter of sherry, the glasses and plate of plain biscuits or simple but delicious canapés, the cocktails, shaken up and ready to be poured *at once.*

There isn't anyone who can walk onto a stage-set like that without involuntarily stopping to exclaim, "But how *lovely!*"

And that, of course, is just what you want.

All this should be in readiness at the first ring of the bell. No dashing around to light the candles and the fire after the guests arrive. A hostess I know simply won't learn this. You come into her chilly living room and look wistfully at the lifeless hearth. "Would you like the fire lighted?" she asks politely. "Oh no," you say quickly, knowing that is the reply she hopes you will make. And you and she and the other guests sit about with the uncomfortable feeling of waiting for the party to begin.

Though keeping the homelike atmosphere of your living room as the most charming setting for your party, the room should be completely in order and immaculate in all its details. The brass of andirons and fender, brass furniture handles and other fittings should positively gleam. Glass lamps and vases and other objects should be polished. The fireplace, in summer when you can't possibly give yourself an excuse for having a fire, can have two or three white-birch logs laid on the well-polished andirons and some pleated white shelf paper made into a fan. Paint the inside of the fireplace a shiny black or dead white. Don't leave it red or yellow brick. Paint the hearth shining black or dull white. I know a woman who put a huge Boston fern in her fireplace in summer with a small electric fan behind it to keep the leaves moving.

If you are careful about all these details your room will have that well-groomed look without which beauty does not come into its own and which brings much that falls below the standard of beauty a good deal closer to perfection. This means elbow grease and not money (no alibis).

If you're giving a large party, and of course if it is a buffet meal in which the living room is to be the dining room, too, then it will be necessary to rearrange some of the furniture to make groupings so that a number of people can talk together cozily. You will probably have to fit in a number of small extra chairs. You will also need a number of small low tables—at least one to every two chairs. As a general rule I think every comfortable armchair should have its own small table, either before it or beside it. If it stands beside the chair it should be exactly the same height as the end tables that flank your sofa.

Most coffee tables are too high and too teetery. Very few of them are as big as they well might be. Ideally the table before the sofa should be just a *little lower* than the seat of the sofa. They can even be almost as long as the sofa itself.

And again I repeat, keep your upholstered furniture balanced as to height and mass. The result is a room which will always be in harmony, even when you bring into it the extra chairs and tables you require for a large number of guests. As for those extra tables, why not get several nests of them of unfinished wood? You can buy these inexpensively in any large department store. Most of these are too tall. Be severe with a saw, paint them (perhaps black and gold, or the color that will match the walls of your living room). Store them in a corner of the room or a closet and bring them out when you are having a party.

Naturally you will see that plenty of ash trays are provided within easy reach. And that these are taken out, emptied, washed and replaced once or twice during the evening. (Though it's positively amazing how many hostesses slip up on this.) If there is no maid to attend to this as part of her duty then do it yourself, as unobtrusively as possible. Or train your husband to take it on as one of his duties as host. You won't have to go to the bother of washing and polishing the trays after you have emptied them if you provide yourself with duplicates which can be brought in as the dirty ash trays are taken out.

Get the big, smart-looking ash trays made of clear glass. Have the cigarettes in glass boxes and plenty of matches done up in smart-looking packets with your initials or the name of your house printed on them.

Above all, look carefully to the lighting of your rooms. Think of the pains a stage director is at to light his stage and every character on it. Lighting is an art. A lot can be done with it. Lamps are tremendously important, and so are lamp shades. *Lamps date a room as nothing else can.* Usually they are too small in size. Remember that lamps should be large, placed low, with large, smart, but plain-looking shades. Try lining your lamp shades with pale pink and see what a becoming light this throws over the room and all who are in it. Send your electric-light brackets to the nearest thrift shop.

A friend of mine who entertains a good deal tells me that when she gives an evening party she always puts one blue daylight bulb in each of her double- or triple-socket lamps. The jewelers use these bulbs to light their displays. My friend says that it gives a most becoming light and one that all women look well in.

The living room needs to be well and softly lighted throughout. The dining room, on the other hand, is more effective when all the light is concentrated on the table and on those gathered about it, leaving the rest of the room shadowy. This trick lighting tends to draw the group about the table closer. I've often noticed, too, that it has the effect of making conversation more spirited.

And that, too, is what you are after.

## If They Go Upstairs

IF YOU HAVE A POWDER ROOM downstairs where the women guests can leave their wraps and prink for a moment before a well-lighted mirror this is a great advantage at party times. If not, then the women guests will have to go upstairs either into a guest room or into your own room.

Be sure that powder, extra hairpins, comb and tissues are ready on the dressing table and fresh towels and new guest soap in the adjoining bathroom. Have a vase of fresh flowers on your dressing table.

If it is your room and bath which must be used for this purpose this means getting yourself and your husband dressed and out of them and both in apple-pie order before the guests arrive. *It means that everything of a personal nature is out of sight.*

## Take a Last-Minute Look Around

THERE'S NOTHING SO ESSENTIAL to your composure as having the final ten minutes before the party breaks for a last-minute survey of yourself, your house and all the preparations for the party. Go through the rooms and see that you have not missed one of the small but ever-so-important details we have been talking about.

1. Is the lighting right outside the house? In the living room? In the dining room?
2. Is the piano tuned and invitingly open? Is there some music ready to hand?
3. Is the radio tuned in to the right station for music that won't interfere with conversation?
4. Are the cocktails and sherry, with ice, glasses and canapés ready on their little table in the living room?
5. How about the cigarettes? Matches? Ash trays?

6. Are unusual or foreign magazines placed where a guest can pick one up and perhaps start an interesting conversation?

7. Are the family pets ready to play their part as hosts?

8. Are the children, if they are old enough, ready to say how-do-you-do to your friends before going upstairs? If too young to appear at the party are they safely tucked in bed?

9. Is the fire lighted? And the candles?

10. Are the curtains drawn snugly to give the room the feeling of being well enclosed against the night? Or, if it is summer, are the windows invitingly open onto the terrace and light turned on outside to give a glimpse of the garden?

Ah, there's a crunch of wheels on the gravel of the drive. There's just time for a quick, last-minute look at *yourself*. The curtain is going up. Your party is about to begin.

## HOW MRS MERRYWELL FOUND OUT THAT THE SECRET OF SUCCESS MAY BE A COMPROMISE

For three years Mrs Merrywell had told herself at intervals that next spring—or next September, at latest—they would have the living room done over. Goodness knows, it needed it. A tall lanky husband who liked to stretch out while he read the evening paper and two sturdy, freckled sons who never seemed to move without a dog at their heels hadn't left much of the living-room rug, furniture or hangings. Mrs Merrywell, who was small and dainty, sighed over this frequently. She would have loved a cool, exquisite, impersonal sort of room with white fur rugs on the dark, polished floor and a Chippendale cabinet filled with the bits of Lowestoft her godmother had left her. A room which would be beautiful by candlelight. In short, what she wanted was the romantic touch.

Have You —

flowers?

cigarettes?

pairs of lamps?

ash trays?

new magazines?

good cheer?

music?

and a bright fire?

Jas.

What she had was realism. A sofa worn into hollows where small el-
bows and knees had burrowed. A table in one corner heaped with wires,
glass jars and bits of copper and string which represented Mr Merrywell's
and the boys' efforts at television. Piles of dog-eared books and magazines
too precious to be thrown away, muddy footprints—boys' and dogs' . . .

Of course if they could have afforded a larger house in which there
would be a family living room and a drawing room too . . . But they
couldn't, and that was *that*.

Regretfully Mrs Merrywell gave up the idea of a room that would be
a setting for her. Instead she determined to create one which would be a
setting for the family. An Early American room, with pine-paneled
walls, with pieces of fine, sturdy old furniture and a break front in which
to place some choicely bound books and the precious Lowestoft. A portrait over the mantel . . .

On her days in town Mrs Merrywell haunted the American wing of
the Metropolitan Museum. She got estimates on paneling the room in
Georgia pine. She and Jim began to save up for this. They figured that by
going without a new fur coat and cutting down on vacation trips they
might be able to have the pine-paneled room in a year or two.

One day when Mrs Merrywell was lunching with her sister in town
and telling Belle everything she had done since the last time they were together her sister demanded: "Don't you and Jim ever ask any people to
the house any more?"

Mrs Merrywell hedged. "We're out of the way of it, I guess. Jim likes
to play with the boys. And young Jim had that nasty throat, you remember."

Her sister tilted her Lily Dache hat a shade more over her left eye.

"Alibis." She sniffed. "It's that living room of yours. You're ashamed of it. That's why you don't entertain. Why don't you have it done over?"

"We're going to." And rapturously Mrs Merrywell described her plans for the pine-paneled room.

"When?" her sister demanded.

"Next year. Or the year after. You've no idea, Belle, what pine-paneling costs."

Belle was obviously not impressed. "If you wait till the year after next to ask your friends to the house you won't have any friends to invite. They'll all think you've taken the veil or gone psychopathic or something. I can see I've taken you in hand only just in time. How much money have you saved for the room?"

Mrs Merrywell told her.

"Good. We'll go right out and spend it."

Ten minutes later Mrs Merrywell found herself in a shop being shown a wallpaper which cleverly simulated pine paneling and which was breath-takingly inexpensive, looking at lengths of reproduction of English chintz and choosing one with big red roses and green leaves on a white ground. After that they ordered an inexpensive gay rug of light crimson red. Later, in another shop, low black-lacquer-and-gold tables, a pine mantel of lovely design and an unfinished corner cupboard of good early colonial lines. "Your carpenter can fit it into the corner of the room and finish it to match the mantel and the wall paper," Mrs Merrywell's sister explained. "Paint the inside of it to match the roses in the chintz or the green of the leaves. That will set off your Lowestoft beautifully."

In November the Merrywells gave a housewarming when their living room was finished. They asked dozens of people, old and young. They lighted the room with lots of tall white candles, looped the mantel and the portrait above it with ropes of laurel leaves which the boys made for the purpose. They carried in a log of apple wood, from an abandoned farm out in the country, and made a ceremony of lighting the first fire on the new hearth. Belle sent out a great stack of music, all old songs which most of the guests had sung in their youth and were eager to sing again. They had an enormous bowl of hot punch with spiced apples floating in it, made from a recipe famous on the eastern shore of Maryland, and doughnuts. They rolled back the rugs and danced the lancers and a Virginia reel.

It was a wonderful party. "When are you going to do this again?" everyone asked.

Of course you can't repeat a housewarming. But the Merrywells do have several big, jolly, old-fashioned general parties every year. Sometimes Mrs Merrywell entertains at a buffet supper in her "pine-paneled room," using little tables for her guests, that she has stained and waxed to look like the paneled walls. She has the satisfaction of knowing that Mr Merrywell, the boys, the dogs and she, herself, seem to belong in it.

# 3

# WHAT KIND OF ENTERTAINING SUITS YOU?

## Be Yourself

YOUR TASTE IN PARTIES tells the world as much about you as your taste in hats.

Are you one of those who think it's fun to celebrate a really stupendous snowfall by ringing up half a dozen friends and going for a sleigh ride and coming home to a piping hot supper by a roaring fire?

Do you ever gather twenty or thirty people of all ages for an evening of charades, with fruit and cheese and beer to follow the fun?

Do you seize on a big football game which is to be broadcast to give a cocktail party at that hour, with a radio turned on in each room and plenty of comfortable chairs (also cushions on the floor) so everyone can listen to the game and enjoy their drinks luxuriously?

Do you like to plan a fancy-dress party, with everyone coming dressed as they were on the happiest moment of their lives (a friend of mine did this), or in dirndls and leather shorts and Tyrolean hats for an Austrian party, or in some other amusing or picturesque costume?

If you feel like doing any one of these things, or something original and entirely different, *do it*. Don't put it off until you've bought a new car, or have more money, or a bigger house or until you know more people. None of these are valid excuses. They're alibis.

Stop alibying. Give yourself the sort of party you long for *right now*.

Some people are at their best at big parties; others shine in a small, intimate group. Whichever your type is live up to it. If you know that you are at your best presiding over an informal but carefully planned small dinner at which you can direct the conversation so that each of your chosen guests has a chance to express himself, then make that your favorite manner of entertaining. If you know a great many people, and accept invitations from them, then it may be necessary for you to give your famous little dinners at frequent intervals. If you do this really well the first thing you know you will find you have a reputation for clever, smart entertaining.

Perhaps you are like me; I love a "gala" occasionally. By that I mean a fairly large evening party with music and dancing. Three or four card tables can be set out in one room for those who prefer bridge or Chinese checkers or backgammon to talk and dancing. A big party like this, which includes all ages, comes perfectly early in the autumn when everyone has just come back from vacationing. It's fun seeing all one's friends again and in their prettiest clothes. Everyone is eager to see everyone else and to hear what they have been doing. The women usually welcome a chance to wear their new evening dresses. And usually the house has just been freshened up delightfully for the winter.

Also, here's a tip worth remembering. If you know a great many people and want to, or for some reason or other feel that you should, entertain them all (your husband may be running for Congress or he may have been promoted to be head of his department at the university) remember that a "gala," even with music for dancing and lots of flowers for decoration, is easier and even less expensive than a great many small luncheons and dinners.

I have a friend who has a very large visiting list and whose husband's business makes it necessary that she entertain a great deal. For years she has made it a rule whenever she gives a large dinner party to follow it the next day with another party exactly like it. Only the guest list is different. She says she finds it a great convenience (also an economy) to double up on her entertaining in this way. For one thing, the house is all arranged for a large number of guests. The extra chairs, tables, linen, silver and glass are all in readiness. Usually the flowers are as fresh on the second day as when they were arranged for party number one. As everyone knows there are always a lot of the party flourishes—the peppermints and salted almonds, favors, place cards, olives and even wines left over from any party to start off a second performance.

I couldn't do it that way myself. My second party would be wan and tired. It would be entirely lacking in spontaneity. But for a very busy woman in public life, or the wife of an army or naval officer or of a college president or a politician, the plan has its points.

No one wants to have only big parties. Very often a taste for big, pretentious parties with elaborate decorations, expensive refreshments and paid entertainers is a smoke screen for a shy, nervous hostess who is secretly fearful of letting anyone come close enough to know her at all. If you are timid about party giving it's best to come out and face yourself on the matter here and now. Ask yourself if you're going to go through life like a scared rabbit. Or whether the time hasn't come to take this matter up with yourself and find out what kind of entertaining really suits *you?*

The first thing to have absolutely clear in your own mind is why you are giving a party at all. Is it to impress or to compete with someone else? That's a sorry sort of send-off for any party. The game of "keeping up with the Joneses" never works. No matter how hard you try to win there's always another Jones around the corner with a newer, faster, bigger car, who belongs to more clubs, has a bigger house and can give more elaborate parties. Cut your parties to fit your own figure and they will suit you. Because they suit *you*, your friends will be suited too.

Or perhaps you have thought it would be a good idea to give a party to pay back a lot of party debts and other obligations. These are like all other debts; they must be paid. But remember, it's fatal to the success of any party to jumble an odd lot of people together, whose only reason for being together at all is that you have accepted their hospitality at various times. The cleverest hostess in the world can't make a "mop-up" party go. It takes considerable skill to arrange a large number of guests one does not know well into several parties of various sorts, carefully sprinkling them with some old friends who will balance the gatherings.

Here's another value of the "gala." You can ask to it a lot of people you do not know intimately. Too, I have always found that people like to be asked to a large, rather "elegant" party.

Everywhere I go throughout the country I find that most people today find it easier to entertain at an informal buffet luncheon or dinner. This sort of entertaining has superseded every other form of hospitality. Occasionally, I admit, one gets tired of the endless standing around, wait-

ing for all the guests to arrive. One longs for a table in a quiet room, with six chairs around it, six people in them and some real conversation. Later on we shall have a whole chapter devoted to informal entertaining. But here and now I want to say that whether you plan a formal dinner party of ten or twelve or a buffet dinner with thirty guests it is a good thing to have a plan worked out in your mind about seating your guests at the little tables you have provided. Even at a buffet meal, at which the guests serve themselves, I use place cards. I find the party goes better that way. There are no dull groups, no leftovers or wallflowers. The shy people can be fitted into groups of gay, talkative ones, and this way the two most attractive women won't grab all the nicest men.

Place cards are a necessity at a dinner party. Is there anything in the world more agonizing than to stand in a huddle at the dining-room door while your hostess fumbles for a scrap of paper and her glasses?

"Dear me, now wait a minute," she murmurs. "I've got it all down here somewhere. Let me see . . . Mr Green, you go here. Then Mrs Orange . . . No, that's wrong. Mr Green, you belong down at the other end. Miss Pink comes next. Oh dear, that won't do at all. It brings Mr Orange right next his own wife. . . ."

## If Not Bridge, Then What?

MANY WOMEN HAVE ONE RECIPE for giving a successful party. Others have two. The first is bridge, backgammon or other games. The second is dancing. Both may be fun, but when you have been asked to do both with the same people over and over again don't you long for a change?

It is my observation that bridge fans have the endurance of nine-day bicycle racers. They never seem to crave any other entertainment. If you are of this mind and most of your friends are, too, then specialize on bridge. You might do as a friend of mine does; she dedicates Thursday to entertaining. At the beginning of the summer she writes all her women friends that she will be at home every Thursday from eleven in the morning on through the afternoon. She asks them to let her know on the afternoon before they are coming so that she can make her preparations. She lives in the country and is lucky enough to have her own tennis court. The croquet set is laid out for a game. There are bridge tables on the porch. At one o'clock there is a simple buffet luncheon. After that the games go on without any of the fuss or chatter that spoil the usual bridge party for serious players.

Bridge fans want other players who match them in skill or stakes. They won't thank you for giving them Aunt Caroline for a partner just because the party is being given for her, unless Aunt Caroline plays a keen game. They want all the equipment for the game ready to hand: good light, chairs of the right height with comfortable backs; cigarettes and ash trays; a long drink of iced fruit juice, iced tea or plain water during the playing and quiet in which to concentrate on the business in hand. After the score has been made you can lead the way into another room for tea or other drinks.

But it is quite likely that a number of your bridge-playing friends have not yet reached this state of oblivion to every other sort of entertainment. These might find it fun to be asked to meet you for dinner at some out-of-the-way foreign restaurant in your city. Or at an attractive inn within easy driving distance. Your party there would have the delicious charm of unexpectedness.

However, don't leave the unexpectedness to chance. Make sure of it by going to the restaurant on the day before the party. Enter into consultation with the manager and even with the chef. Find out if the latter has not a special dish he makes superlatively. Choose your table and its fittings and flowers. With all these details attended to you can drive up three minutes before your guests arrive, in perfect peace of mind.

After dinner take the party back to your home for more coffee and liqueurs, for talk and music. It's ten to one they won't miss the bridge. They will have had too much fun going somewhere and doing something that is "different."

## If You're Musical

Suppose you are not a bridge fan but an ardent music lover. You can build your parties around that. Choose an evening when a specially fine program is to be broadcast, perhaps a Toscanini concert. Ask your music-loving friends for that hour. Make the radio or victrola the center of the room. Get an amplifier.

Draw around it your comfortable chairs. Some may prefer cushions on the floor or low canvas deck chairs. The low glow of a quiet fire, candlelight, cigarettes and drinks within easy reach, and then the music. . . .

After the broadcast there is the fun of discussing it with other music lovers.

You can have fun with all the quiz programs that come over the air if you will get a group together with pencils and papers to answer the questions as they are out. Have a prize for the winner and a booby prize for the one who thinks Bach is spelled with a "K" and Handel is something that turns a barrel organ.

Perhaps you are keen about politics. Then why not give a dinner on the evening when there is to be an important political speech or debate? Or for the Thursday night Town Meeting of the Air? Lead the conversation at dinner round to the subject to be discussed. Get your guests to express their own views. This won't be hard when it's a current issue. The speech itself will come in patly after such discussion, and after it is over it is interesting to see what opinions have changed. (If any.)

The radio provides innumerable themes for parties. Don't pass up the chance to give your husband a party on the night there is to be a big prize fight. Ask in several of his friends; provide plenty of his favorite drinks, large, man-sized sandwiches, tables for poker or bridge. After greeting the guests retire unobtrusively to a luxurious evening in bed with an entertaining book. There is no need to feel neglected or left out. Give yourself a party feeling by having flowers in your room, wearing your loveliest bed jacket and knowing that the evening is doing wonders for your complexion and your nerves.

Your hobbies, and your husband's, are excellent starters in the way of entertaining. Particularly if these are shared by your friends.

## If You Live in the Suburbs

IF SO, THEN YOU MAY SUFFER from the problem which most suburbanites confront. You have a split acquaintance. This can be almost as disturbing as a split personality. In fact, it frequently leads to one.

Half of your friends live in the same neighborhood with you. The other half live in town. Your friendships in the first group are based on community interests, on belonging to the same country club, on having your children in the same schools. Your friends in town are leftovers from the days before you married or moved to the suburbs. You see your neighbors so often that there is no novelty and very little excitement about having them come to the house. You see your friends in town only in hurried snatches. In consequence you feel sometimes that it is difficult to pick up the threads with them. If you could just juggle the two groups together; let one balance the other.

Well, why not? True, city dwellers don't feel like taking a commuters' train out to dinner in the suburbs with the prospect of taking a late train back. But instead of planning an evening party why not have a late Sunday lunch? All the husbands and extra men are available then. And usually they are in a better frame of mind and nerves than after a hard day at their offices. The suburbanites will welcome a change in the regulation Sunday routine. And city dwellers usually enjoy a chance to go out of town for a few hours on a Sunday.

Plan the luncheon hour to agree with the arriving train schedule. Have drinks ready for out-of-towners and the near-bys the minute they arrive. See that everybody meets everyone. Remember you planned this party to mend that split in your acquaintance. Nothing is accomplished if the neighbors get into a huddle over the affairs of the Greens Committee and the out-of-towners are engrossed in hearing the news of Clare's second trip to Reno.

Whisk them all in to lunch, which may be served from a buffet and should combine the qualities of breakfast and lunch, with no hint of the old-fashioned, heavy Sunday dinner.

After lunch, which could consist of a hot soup from a large tureen, cold roast beef or cold chicken, a mixed vegetable salad, baked potatoes and a simple dessert, everyone can explore, make friends with the children, meet the pets, go for a walk to some point of local interest, play shuffleboard or ping-pong or tennis, swim or just sit and talk. Early tea and cocktails will start them all off in time for the out-of-towners to catch a fiveish (don't urge them to stay later) train back to the city (rested and refreshed, we hope).

If you live near a country club there are always tennis or golf tournaments that you can turn into delightful parties. Get some of your friends together for lunch, then go on to the tournament. Many sports lovers live in town and would adore being asked to such a party as this. It might be the perfect way to entertain your husband's boss and his wife. Or your sister-in-law's sister and her husband. And don't pass over your unmarried women friends when it comes to a party such as this. They would much rather be asked to lunch and see the tennis finals, particularly if your husband can bring up some unattached men for the party, than to be put down for bridge or a big general cocktail party.

## Where Do Ideas Come From?

IF YOU LOVE TO GIVE PARTIES you will find ideas for them in all sorts of places.

One young couple had been racking their brains as to how to entertain the members of a quite high-brow club to which they belonged. Then they took a motor trip through New England during October and came home with the idea of having an old-fashioned husking-bee party.

The house was decorated with cornstalks and big yellow pumpkins. Each woman guest was given a pink-and-white-checked gingham apron and a matching sunbonnet. The men guests were fitted with wide-brimmed straw hats. These very dignified and quite formal elderly men and women were a bit startled at first, then the costumes got in their work and everybody unbent and began to have a good time.

The host, who had a fine voice, and some friends of his had gotten up a program of early American folk songs which they sang delightfully. There was a fiddler to play old harvest tunes. And the party ended by everyone dancing the old square dances that are such fun.

## An Austrian Party

SEVERAL YEARS AGO some friends and I spent some time in Austria. A village fete that we saw and took part in that summer gave us the idea for a dinner dance which turned out to be one of the loveliest and most successful parties ever given.

My friends and I tried to re-create for our friends as much as we could of the spirit and atmosphere of that fete in the Tyrolean village.

We chose an evening just before Christmas for the party which was to begin as a dinner dance and last as long as anyone wished to stay.

At that time I was living in my house which had a large high-ceilinged room wonderful for parties. There was a big Georgian fireplace and a high Palladium window looking out on a rhododendron garden enclosed with a high brick wall.

We asked everyone to come in Austrian costume, the women in dirndls with flower headdresses; the men in leather shorts, fancy suspenders over white shirts and amusing Tyrolean hats.

On the night of the party we all gathered in the dining room on the floor above the big room for cocktails. Then at a signal the band downstairs struck up a lively Austrian march. We formed a procession, single file, each one holding the lighted candles, and marched down the stairs and round and round the room, forming a snake dance of moving lights.

Along one side of the room, nearly covering it, was a large tapestry. Before this was a long narrow table with benches on each side, seating about twenty. Each end of the table was lighted with great candelabras, giving the appearance of an Austrian inn—with a red-and-white-checked tablecloth and, down the center, hemlock boughs and pine cones covered with tinsel. Tables for six stood all around the room, leaving an open space in the middle for dancing.

There was an amateur Austrian band consisting of Austrian workmen and shopkeepers who played together for the love of it and to make money when they could. We felt terribly proud of having discovered them. The band had tremendous *élan* and enjoyed the party as much as the guests. They all came in their Tyrolean dress and brought their wives or best girls with them (the women were in costume too). They all sang rollicking songs, and the guests joined in the chorus and danced some of their gay, elaborate folk dances for us. We could all join in some of these like the one in which everyone stands in a circle, holding hands. One couple dances round and round in the middle of the circle. Then each partner takes a pillow. The girl puts hers on the floor before one of the men in the circle; she kneels on it and so does he. They touch cheek to cheek and then get up and dance. Meanwhile her first partner has chosen another girl in the same way. So the dance goes on, adding couples all the time until everyone is dancing. Naturally, as the evening goes on and the wine with it, the gaiety grows gayer and gayer.

That party was really a lot of fun. My friend, Mrs Charlie Marshall, had cut a lot of big hearts out of red cardboard and had written mottoes on them in tinsel. We used these as favors. They had silver ribbons to hang them around the neck. There were other hearts made out of gingerbread and iced with colored sugar, like the ones we had bought during the fete in that Tyrolean village.

The guests entered into the spirit of the thing by doing all sorts of stunts. One of these was a witty play which our friends, Marjorie and Fair Osborn, wrote and acted, along with Charlie Lawrence, the inventor of the engine which took Lindbergh across the Atlantic. It was all amusing burlesque, one feature of which Charlie Towne played the part of a baby in an enormous wicker bassinet, with knitted bootees on his fists which he waved in the air like the baby's feet.

Of course the costumes helped to make the fun. Some of the women were lovely in their dirndls and embroidered aprons and lots of ribbons, tinsel, flowers and jewels in their hair. I had a headdress of cornflowers with silver and great long diamond peasant earrings and an effective necklace (paste, of course), which I wore with my dirndl with huge muslin puffed sleeves.

One man who had just returned to town that day and had no costume came in checked trousers rolled up to his knees, extravagant garters holding up his socks and a brief case hung on his back, with a woman's corselet garter peeping out of it. Three others came as Alpine climbers with very tall alpenstocks tied with bunches of real flowers and with great coils of rope that tied them together. Elsa Maxwell, I remember, came dressed like a man, in leather shorts and an embroidered white shirt and flowered suspenders.

But it was the beauty of the party, I believe, that everyone felt most of all and which everyone has remembered. People still talk about it.

And I shall never forget the color, the gaiety, the evergreen boughs, the songs, the candlelight and firelight, the laughter and the red paper hearts—nor looking out through the window at the snow flakes drifting down through the night.

## Why Don't I Do Any of These Things?

WELL, WHY DON'T YOU? Do you tell yourself that your house is too small and not planned for entertaining? Or that your budget won't let you? Nonsense! Those aren't excuses. They're alibis.

Do you say: "I will when Bill makes more money," or, "After we've had the living room redecorated," or, "When little Ann is bigger, then I'll start in to entertain and see my old friends and make new ones."

Alibis again.

These are the promptings of that Will to Be Dreary psychologists tell us about. It's that little imp locked away in your subconscious that is teasing you into believing that it's too hard or too expensive or too much bother to give a party. And yet, all the time, part of you knows that a party is exactly what you need for your morale.

True, it isn't easy to entertain in a house with a dining room that's a tight squeeze for six and where eight people can only get in with the help of a shoehorn. Yet it can be done delightfully. I know many who do it again and again. But if you'd rather not why not take your guests to dinner at the club or at an inn—even a funny little inexpensive one—and then return to the house for coffee, drinks, conversation and fun.

Or what about that stretch of smooth lawn under the apple tree? A tea table with a purring kettle would look charming set there. And little Ann, in a pink linen sunbonnet playing in her sand pile, would be entertainment enough for several of your mother's and mother-in-law's friends who have entertained you.

If you live in a tiny apartment in the city you may have a roof with a quite stupendous view. Sunday morning breakfast on the terrace, all cooked electrically, is an ideal way to entertain three or four. Try it on your new friends and watch the effect.

## Capitalize What You Have

THAT'S ONE INFALLIBLE RULE. Perhaps your asset is a stretch of beach where you can have a clam roast and a swimming party, or a shack in the woods not too far to go out to for moonlight picnic suppers. You might equip your camping site with permanent tables and benches and carry along with you when you picnic several comfortable folding canvas chairs.

Some relations of mine did over an old boathouse by a lake for parties. They stained the walls and the peaked wooden ceiling a deep brown, put in some deep sofas covered in a bright yellow woolen fabric, installed a big Franklin stove and hung a collection of Currier and Ives prints on the dark walls. A built-in closet is equipped with dozens of tin plates, big earthenware mugs for beer (for coffee too), forks, knives and spoons with green handles (from the ten-cent store) and games of every sort.

There is never any need of carrying out anything from the house (except food) whenever they give a picnic supper. And the husband has solved that problem by buying a child's express wagon (a big one), painting it red and yellow and green like a peasant farm cart, in which he can *pull* the picnic from the house kitchen to the picnickers on the beach.

They have really big parties in their boathouse, for everyone loves to come to them. And everyone says they have the very best hamburgers, doughnuts, coffee and deep-dish blueberry pies.

## Moonlight on the Water

NOT LONG AGO I heard about a party which seems to me about as near perfection as most of us ever come in this existence.

A couple, living in Pennsylvania not far from one of the old canals which thread the eastern part of the state, rented a canal boat and a strong white horse for an evening when there was to be a full moon.

The deck of the barge was carefully hosed off and dried. The guests were asked to bring along extra cushions and rugs to supplement all those their hosts had gathered together for the party.

The guests arrived in the late-summer dusk. Drinks were served and everyone went down to the canal and aboard the barge. The driver clucked to his horse, and the boat began to move slowly through the calm water.

As the dusk deepened and the stars came out they rode several miles and at the lock they found a picnic supper waiting for them. (It had been sent on ahead in the host's station wagon.) Later they made the return journey when the full moon was coming up over the trees that bordered the towpath. It made a shining path of light along the water. It was almost *too* romantic and beautiful for words.

One of the guests was a very, very famous singer. (It was beautiful Lucrezia Bori.) She stood up in the boat's bow, with the moonlight full on her; she sang one aria after another with no other accompaniment than the soft plash of water against the sides of the barge.

Of course it's only once in a blue moon that a beautiful, romantic party like this one could happen. But my point is, it *did* happen. And because two people had the sensitive imagination and the desire to bring it into being. And because they cleverly made use of what they had close at hand to create an evening of beauty that everyone who shared it (or those who merely heard about it, like myself) will remember always.

The recipe for a perfect party: take what you've got; mix well with imagination, courage, a dash of humor and the desire to enjoy life. The result is guaranteed to please.

## CASE HISTORY OF A LADY WHO CONQUERED HER MOTHER–IN–LAW

Young Mrs M—— knew her mother-in-law did not like her. At least not much. Old Mrs M—— was too well-bred and too fond of her son not to try to conceal her disappointment that John should have been the first member of the M—— family in seven generations to marry outside the sacred precincts of Massachusetts. Why, old Mrs M—— said to herself every day (as young Mrs M—— shrewdly suspected), couldn't John have married a girl he'd known since his dancing-school days and not a perfect stranger who came from—of all places in the world—Arizona?

John and his wife joked about it sometimes. John thought it was funny. But young Mrs M—— didn't. She knew it was important that John's mother and John's wife should like each other, and she did her level best to bring this about.

For six months she curbed her Western accent and her Western ways. She studied the ways of the Massachusetts town which John's colonial ancestor had founded, and tried to do likewise. She learned the hour considered proper for going marketing and the time for having all the shutters closed at night. She was careful to buy her bread from the right shop and to serve all the sacred New England dishes. When she entertained she was as meticulous as a Japanese craftsman in copying all the details from the local model she selected.

She didn't see how Mrs M—— could still consider her odd or dangerous in any way. But she knew that Mrs M—— did. There was that *something* in the old lady's eye.

One October morning young Mrs M—— received a telephone call. (No Western man ever writes letters.) Her brother Tom was in New York. He was coming right up to Massachusetts to see her.

"And trot out all your New England fillies, sis," he ordered. "I want to see the whole Mayflower strain."

From the force of six months' habit young Mrs M—— was starting to telephone to order the approved mold of ice cream, the conventional flowers, vegetables and other party appurtenances. The idea of Tom in such a setting made her sit down on the lowest step of the stairs and laugh till she cried.

After that she wiped her eyes, spent ten minutes with a paper and pencil, did some telephoning such as she had not done since her marriage and then began to gather up guests.

"This is Tom's and *my* kind of party for once," she told herself. "It isn't old Mrs M——'s."

Dinner was served out of doors. There was a long table spread with a rough linen cloth (in fact, several tables put together), lighted by hurricane lamps. There were clay casseroles of chile con carne and real *tortillas*. The last John brought out from a Mexican restaurant in Boston.

There was also a big roast of beef from which John cut the slices. There was a cunningly mixed and artfully seasoned salad. And a delicious dessert made from persimmons. Down under a tree in the garden was a man with a banjo who knew all the cowboy songs. Tom had a fine baritone.

The songs and stories brought something exciting to the quiet New England setting.

Tom was an instant success with the Mayflower strain. The girls John might have married understood for the first time why he preferred young Mrs M—— to any of them. "Don't you see? She strikes him the way that brother of hers strikes us."

And old Mrs M——, caught in the act of joining in the chorus of "Git along, little dogies," actually smiled at her daughter-in-law. She began that very evening telling people how clever John's wife is. And how unusual.

Last winter old Mrs M—— wrote the American Express Company for folders about trips to the Southwest. John said to his wife: "I wouldn't be surprised if she came home in a ten-gallon hat."

# 4

# INFORMAL ENTERTAINING

## Fun Without Fuss

I HAVE BEEN TOLD that no woman can possibly be entertaining to others if she can't entertain herself, all by herself. Does the prospect of an evening alone give you the blues? Can you look forward to a week end without any invitations or engagements without any premonition of boredom? If you can then you are well on the way toward being an entertaining person. In other words, a good hostess.

If you can't—and really, it's surprising how terrified a lot of us are of our own company—then it's high time you discovered the fun of entertaining yourself. Informally, of course. Only an Alice-in-Wonderland would consider sending herself an invitation to dinner, carefully worded in the third person singular.

But ask yourself to dine delightfully nonetheless. No hasty, pickup meal. Plan your dinner as carefully as if you were planning to entertain your best beau. Light the candles and the fire if it is winter. If it is summer plan to dine on the porch by an open window with a view. Dress in something pretty and becoming. Set your tray with a lovely cloth—white, pale pink or pale yellow linen—your prettiest china and glass and a tiny vase of flowers. Indulge yourself with a menu that you enjoy—cold, jellied madrilene, breast of chicken, a delicious salad, fruit or even a dash of dessert if you aren't counting calories. In short, why not make a party out of being by yourself?

After dinner there is the radio to entertain you. Or if you are lucky enough to have an orthophonic turn it on and enjoy some of your favorite music. Go through several of the latest magazines. Read the article you have been promising yourself you would read when you had time and knew you would not be interrupted, or settle down on the sofa with an exciting new novel. Don't do chores. This evening is for fun.

At the end of an evening spent in this way you will go to bed and drop off to sleep with a happy feeling. That direful Will to Be Dreary will not have gotten in any of its work. You will not have suffered the effects of the poison of loneliness or self-pity. Instead you will feel that you have been an honored and enjoyable guest. That, in itself, will make you look and feel when you wake positively *years* younger.

## Two Is Company

BEST OF ALL, of course, the real fun is entertaining just one person. It may be someone you do not know well but believe you would like to know better, or it may be a childhood friend with whom you want the fun of reminiscing for an evening. Whoever it is, the charm for such a party is intimacy.

This is the time for the tea table by the fire. If the meal is to be dinner then do not serve this in the dining room where you and your guest are uncomfortably conscious of being just two people in a room arranged for a larger number. Instead, have a card table set up in the living room or on the porch. Plan your color scheme in table decoration as carefully as if you were entertaining a large dinner party. Choose flowers that are small and fragrant—lilies of the valley, white daisies with six dark red roses, or sweet-smelling freesia.

The menu should be short, simple and simply delicious. Every dish should count. Think of a dinner, for instance, of purée Mongole, fried soft-shell crabs (if you live where you can get them) with tartare sauce, hot roasted squabs with watercress salad, and for dessert half a pineapple, scooped out and filled with pineapple ice. And really soft macaroons.

If you want to be really festive there is nothing that looks more enticing than a wine cooler filled with ice and a small bottle of champagne, sauterne or chablis peeping out of this, waiting to be opened. (You can use American brands of these, of course.)

Consider carefully the color effect of your linen, china, glass and silver. Try a combination of a turquoise-blue linen cloth with flame-pink camellias, white china and candles in candlesticks of clear glass; or perhaps you have picked up some blue Staffordshire or old Canton china plates in your antique-collecting days. Try these on a mustard-yellow cloth with a big bunch of bluets or purple violets.

If you are going to dine out of doors or in front of an open window use straw mats on the bare table, brown and orange (or bright red) pottery and a wooden bowl and wooden plates for the salad course.

It is by just such means that the impression is conveyed to your guest that he (or she) has been paid the greatest of all compliments—that of

being invited for himself alone. Much as everyone likes the excitement
of a big party, there is something especially heart-warming about a little
intimate evening *à deux*. When your hostess has obviously taken pains
to make every detail of the evening perfect you can't help feeling flattered
and pleased.

The same rule of careful attention to the details, simplicity, few courses (but each one of these deliciously prepared and attractively served) applies to the small informal luncheons or dinners you give. Your friends will be quick to appreciate the fact that you have tried to give them a good time. Moreover, they'll have a good time, and so will you.

## Let Everyone Help

ONE ENORMOUS ADVANTAGE that the small informal party has over the big one is that at the former everyone has a chance to do something to help make the party go. It may be a parlor trick after dinner or a new game which everyone is eager to learn; it may be music or an amusing story. It may just be giving the hostess a helping hand with the drinks. Whatever it is, you may be sure that anyone who plays an active role in the party has a lot more fun.

Suppose you know someone who has mastered the secret of making *crêpes suzettes*. Naturally, he (it may very well be a man) adores doing this, since he does it superlatively well. Why not ask him to dinner with three or four of your other friends and give him the fun of cooking the dessert in an electric chafing dish on the table? If it isn't convenient to make the *crêpes* themselves at the table these may be made in advance in the kitchen. (You can buy excellent ones in cans.) But your friend will enjoy preparing the sauce in the chafing dish, and all the others at the party will enjoy watching him and then eat the sauce with approbation.

Whatever form of entertaining you decide to go in for, keep within your resources. If your living room is dining room as well don't choke it up with a big table set for a dinner party. Let your friends sit about the room comfortably and give each one one of the small tables we've talked about, which can be put out of the way after the meal. If you are putting yourself through a period of financial retrenchment make a feature of thrift. You can do it amusingly. Use tablecloths and napkins of paper—the red-and-white-checked ones give the effect of a foreign sidewalk restaurant. Comb the useful five-and-ten-cent stores for smart, pretty—and cheap—china and glass, and plan a menu which costs no more than fifty cents per person. Add another twenty cents per person for a half gallon of a California red and a half gallon of a California white wine, and place decanters filled with these on the tables for guests to serve themselves.

If you use card tables for the dinner these can be cleared and then used to play Chinese checkers, bridge or the new Cuban gambling game you brought back from the last cruise you took.

## Two Women's Ways

THE GREAT THING is to have no effort evident when you ask your friends to come to the house for fun. In this connection I think of two women I know and the contrast they present. One is the wife of a brilliant young lawyer. She and her husband came to New York from a small town upstate. The husband is building up his business and it happens that most of his clients are men with a good deal of money and who live luxuriously. Far more luxuriously than the lawyer and his wife live. When they entertain the wife tries to do in a small apartment, and with one maid, what her husband's clients do in their large houses with a staff of well-trained servants. There's an anxious little pucker between the wife's brows. She finds it impossible to concentrate on her dinner partner because her mind is on the soufflé and the maid. The maid looks harassed and resentful. (You have a feeling she is going to give notice next morning.) The party which started very well with cocktails served by the host in the living room dies away feebly before the attempt at overelaborate food comes on the table. It's simply that nobody can stand the hostess's strain.

The other woman is Lydia J——. Her husband is an assistant editor on one of the national magazines. His salary is not large, and as he and Lydia are buying a farm in Connecticut they have worked out a careful budget and keep rigorously within it. This does not mean that they have cut out having friends, and a lot of new acquaintances, too, to the house. On the contrary, Lydia economizes by having no maid at all. Except the services of a cleaning woman twice a week. She has a shelf of cookbooks which she studies as persistently as she studied the textbooks on political science when working for her degree. Last winter she took a six-weeks' course at a cooking school. Lydia's dinner parties, which she serves on card tables set about her one big room, are beginning to make history in New York. There are never more than three courses, a rich filling soup or some form of shellfish, a hot dish, into which she throws all her culinary zeal and talent, followed by salad and cheese. Nothing that has to be stirred or cooked at the ultimately final moment. Everything ready and waiting, very hot, on an electric grill from which people serve themselves. Everything that should be very cold ready in the refrigerator. For the drinks she has the best liquor, and always enough. Everyone helps, under Lydia's quietly capable direction and everyone has a good time.

## Large Gatherings

EVEN IF YOU'RE GIVING quite a large party—perhaps you have undertaken to entertain your county political club or the Junior League of your community, and you know they are all coming—there's no need to go into a tail spin. Keep cool. Count your resources. Intelligent planning will get you a lot further than hysteria. What are you giving this party for if not for fun?

## Tea and Cocktails

THE COCKTAIL HOUR is one of our American inventions. We were always slightly envious of the British who have the habit of calling a halt in the day at five o'clock to drink cups of scalding hot tea with milk and to eat lots of slices of very thin bread and butter. The British climate makes a hot drink a necessity at fairly frequent intervals.

A fair proportion of Americans go in for tea. But more and more of them gravitate about five in the afternoon toward the cocktail shaker. A gathering of friends at this hour makes a pleasant break between the working day and the evening. Perhaps that is why this has become the most widely popular way of entertaining in America.

The first requisite for such a party is good liquor. The second is plenty of it. Don't try substituting the second recommendation for the first. Lots of people do that, and for that reason lots of men shy away from the cocktails they are offered at parties. They prefer to do their drinking at a bar where they can see the bottle from which their drinks are poured.

*Good liquor is not cheap. Cheap liquor is not good.*

Nor will a lot of very fancy canapés make up for poor drinks. They don't. The whole object of the canapé is to incite the appetite for the drinks. If you promote your guests' thirst and then offer them cocktails of fruit juice, melted ice and a faint tinge of gin all the olives and maraschino cherries in the world won't appease their resentment.

If you're entertaining on a shoestring and have to count the pennies very carefully, then why go in for cocktails at all? Why not be smartly proletarian and have beer on tap or ready to serve from cold bottles, complete with hearty foods? Or, if your friends are connoisseurs of wine, why not have some very good white wine and ask your friends in to try this with some dry, slightly sweet biscuits or sponge cake? Or hunt about for one of the very little known Swedish punches—and these are powerful too. Build your party around this with some really Swedish hors d'oeuvres, arranged as *smörgåsbord*.

But let us say that you have decided to give your friends cocktails, and the best of their kind. The immediate question is *which* kind. At the River Club in New York, as the bartender has told me, the six most popular mixed drinks are: bacardi cocktails, daiquiris, dry martinis, manhattans, old-fashioned cocktails and whisky sours. Usually, and for even a fairly large party, dry martinis, with whisky and soda for highballs, sherry, iced fruit juice and milk for the many who are on diets but who like going to parties just the same, offer something for every taste.

You can mix the martinis just before the party and have them ready to pour onto the cracked ice to be stirred round and round when the guests begin to arrive. Martinis are always stirred, not shaken. An olive is dropped into the glass; the cocktail is poured over it; a thin slice of lemon rind is twisted above the glass to let one drop of the pungent oil fall into it, and the martini is ready.

There's an exact ritual about the glasses for various drinks. Men are proverbially particular about this point. Perhaps you can't honestly feel that it's a life-or-death matter to serve each drink in its properly ordained glass, but probably your husband does. There's nothing for it but to take yourself in hand and learn the ritual and follow it. However, there's no hard-and-fast rule against serving cocktails in champagne glasses, if you like. These hold two drinks at a time, which is a help at a party since it does away with passing and refilling glasses. Too, the champagne glasses seem to make the cocktail even more festive. Even your husband will admit *that*.

Glasses should be brilliantly polished. And none of them should be nicked, even so slightly that the nick can only be felt and not seen. With the accommodating five-and-ten-cent store practically around the corner, you can always replenish your stock of glasses and at small cost. If you have a complete set of very fine glass or crystal—this may have been one of your wedding presents—and several of the pieces are nicked look into the advisability and the cost of having the edges reground. This can be done, and if the glass is really valuable it is worth doing.

My own preference is for clear, uncolored glass. Highball glasses with ships, dolphins and flags painted on them are all well enough on a yacht or at a summer camp, but they seem more suited to college boys' rooms than to a home.

If you are having your friends come to the house for cocktails it is well to have tea, too, since a number of people really prefer it to any other drink during the afternoon. Place the tea tray and service on a low tea table at one end of the living room. Ask one of your friends who has a real feeling for tea to sit there and pour for those who ask for it. At the opposite end of the room have another tray with the cocktail shakers, glasses, bowls of cracked ice, olives and slices of lemon rind. Also have a big pitcher of iced fruit juice and tall glasses. Also a pitcher of cold milk. With the milk I always serve fresh hot gingerbread, of which I am very fond. This plate empties rapidly, I find, proving that there's nothing extraordinary about my taste.

On another table set out a tray with highball glasses, bottles of scotch or rye, or both, a bowl of cracked ice, soda and ginger ale.

What to serve with cocktails? Since Repeal American ingenuity has been at work inventing canapés that cause foreigners to gasp at our temerity. Daring combinations of oysters, peanut butter, caviar, anchovies and melted cheese are set out to betray the unwary into indigestion.

Everyone enjoys something hot to eat with an iced drink. The rule for canapés is the same temperature ruling as applies to all foods: hot things should be *very, very* hot; cold things should be chilled. To keep canapés hot during a long party use a covered oven, such as are used in the clubs and hotels. These are heated by boiling water. If you have an electric heater you can set this out on the sideboard, complete with the various spreads for the squares of toast as prepared. Olives wrapped in bacon and any other hot canapés are kept at the proper temperatures throughout the party in covered dishes preheated in the oven. Place wooden bowls of hot potato chips and of hot nuts where people can reach them easily. Also plates of crisp, raw celery and crunchy fingers of raw carrot, scraped and cut in quarters lengthwise.

The most successful food I serve at my parties are finger rolls. These are cut the long way, buttered and spread with slices of cold turkey or with creamed turkey mince sprinkled with paprika.

Serve only one variety of canapé on a plate, no matter how many plates this makes necessary. Odd collections of various and sundry hors d'oeuvres all on one big plate or tray are too suggestive of a Jumble Sale to be really appetizing. If you want to go in for caviar don't dab a little of this halfheartedly on biscuits or bits of toast and trim it with hard-boiled egg, anchovies or onion. Instead, make a feature of it. Buy a whole pound of caviar (I hope you can afford it) and serve it in a silver bowl set on ice. If you place near this a plate heaped with small pieces of dry toast and some knives people will help themselves and feel that they are being entertained in the grand manner (as indeed they are).

## Buffet Meals

LIKE ALL FASHIONS in everything, from clothes to sports, the buffet meal was started by amateurs. Some smart women decided to try this way of entertaining a large number of people. It was successful, and other women adopted the idea. Today, in a nearly servantless America, entertaining at buffet meals solves a problem which would otherwise keep a lot of us from asking our friends to the house as often as we like.

But even a buffet meal should not be a sort of indoor picnic. Is anyone in the world really comfortable trying to eat while standing up, with a plate in one hand? Or even sitting down, with a plate perched on one knee and a glass on the other?

Even though you are going to serve the food from a buffet, for lunch or dinner, and let people serve themselves, it is my firm conviction that you should set one large or a number of smaller tables, complete with linen, china, glass and silver, and arrange a place for everyone at the party. Seat your guests yourself by arranging place cards. In this way you give the party a good start. There will be no odd, shy, leftover people. After the second course people may change about, but that does not matter. By that time the ice is well broken.

Also with an eye to starting the fun as quickly as possible, it is a good plan to have the *first course on the table at each place when you go into the dining room*. Then people can sit right down and begin to eat and talk. There's none of that awkward standing about and waiting to be served. For this first course you can have cherry-stone clams on the half shell with cocktail sauce and very thin brown-bread sandwiches (but a problem what to do with the ice afterward). Or half a cantaloupe, iced and filled with cold jellied madrilene. Or half an avocado filled with crab-meat mixed with mayonnaise.

In winter serve onion soup in individual covered bowls or oyster stew. Or a soup made of cream of corn with finely shredded crabmeat, seasoned with sherry and paprika. Be sure the tureen (and its cover) are hot before filling it with the soup.

After the first course the men, of course, take away their own and their partner's plates. On the buffet are piles of fresh plates beside the food for the next course. One or two hot dishes, perhaps kidney stew with boiled wild rice, or creamed chicken or turkey, baked macaroni au gratin, or corned-beef hash and baked beans are keeping hot on electric or hot-water plates. Salad is ready in big wooden bowls. A tray holds an assortment of cheeses. For dessert have stewed fruit and a pitcher of custard sauce. Or if the first two courses have not been heavy, a delicious Brown Betty with hard sauce is a good finale. Or cold yoghurt with fresh raspberries.

If your room is large enough you can place the tables around the sides and leave space in the center for dancing during dinner. After all, since you are serving yourselves you can prolong the fun of dining as long as you like and as long as the radio continues to broadcast dance music.

## At Home

IF YOU ARE a business or a professional woman you probably know a great many people and would like to ask them to come to your house occasionally. But there is that problem of time. Your time is your capital. You have to plan your investment of it. Most of us discover sooner or later that we can't run a business and do much going out and entertaining on the same track without paying attention to the signals.

Does this mean that because you have a career you can't have the fun of entertaining? Not at all. Why shouldn't you set apart one late afternoon each week, or if you think you are too busy for that, then one afternoon a month, and let all your friends know that you will be at home then and eager to see them.

When that afternoon comes your living room will be lovely with lots of fresh flowers or greens from the country picked by yourself, lighted candles, a tea table and a table with cocktails and other drinks. You will be looking charming and carefree (you have had a quick bath, ten minutes' rest on the flat of your back with your feet above your head, and you feel like a new woman). All your friends are delighted to see you and to see each other. If you know some musical people there will be one to gravitate to the piano which you have opened temptingly. There may be someone to sing. You never arrange a program. That is too awful. But, as your friends tell you, "At your parties people seem to love to do things."

They do love to when there is welcome and appreciation and the feeling of real hospitality and affection.

One "career" girl I know makes a point of entertaining at breakfast parties on Sunday morning. She specializes in marvelous breakfast dishes:

old-fashioned buckwheat cakes; country sausages and apple fritters; Maryland spoon bread and crisp broiled bacon; corn muffins and popovers which pop like Mauna Loa. Her apartment is tiny; three guests and herself are a perfect fit. In winter breakfast is served on a card table in front of the open fire, in summer by the window which opens onto a small roof. Since she does all her entertaining before lunch this young woman collects pretty and unusual breakfast-table fittings. These enable her to work out a number of charming color schemes in table decoration.

## CASE HISTORY OF THE GIRL WHO COULD GIVE A DINNER FOR EIGHT AND NOT RAISE A RIPPLE

Miss D—— was a career woman. She had a job she adored, a two-room-kitchenette apartment with a real fireplace and, in the offing, a newly acquired bachelor beau named Harvey. It looked like a perfect setup. Miss D—— was not dissatisfied. But sometimes she wished Harvey would make up his mind or something.

Harvey was shy about home life. He clung to his club. Once, when Miss D—— spoke of having some friends in to cocktails or a buffet supper, she noticed that Harvey immediately looked troubled. "Isn't that a lot of bother?" he said. "Why don't you take them out somewhere?"

Gradually, by dint of skillful questions, Miss D—— discovered in Harvey's past a mother who was a fusser. One of those good, conscientious women who make everything they do a trouble and a bore. To Harvey's mother having six friends for dinner had involved overthrowing the family's usual routine for a week.

Harvey, Miss D—— decided, would have to be shown that all women were not like that.

One day she rang him up to tell him that a New York couple whom she had met on a cruise the year before were in town. "I've asked them to dine here. On Thursday. I've asked four other people. And I'm counting on you to help me out."

Harvey accepted but without his usual enthusiasm. "Aren't you going to a lot of trouble?" he demanded. "No," said Miss D—— and smiled as she hung up the receiver.

True to promise, Harvey arrived on Thursday evening a quarter of an hour before the other guests were expected. What he found was as usual: a softly lighted room, a fire of hickory logs blazing on the hearth, candles lighted, pots of flowers (Miss D—— had a friend with a greenhouse) and evergreens everywhere, a table set out with sherry and cocktails and glasses and Miss D—— in a new and most becoming dress, sitting by the fire, looking entirely calm and pleasantly expectant.

Harvey looked surprised. "Have you changed your mind about dining here? Are we going out?"

Miss D—— shook her head.

"Isn't there anything you have to do that I can help with?" he persisted.

"It's all done," said Miss D—— calmly. "If you'll just keep an eye on the fire to see that it burns down to embers. But not *too* far down."

Miss D—— was not too occupied with her other guests not to notice the effect on Harvey when the party got under way. The couple from New York were amusing and friendly. The men set up the iron camp grill when Miss D—— dramatically produced it. (She had bought it for this occasion.) It fitted compactly into the fireplace over the hickory embers. A red casserole filled with macaroni and cheese, already cooked, was brought from the kitchenette and set on one side of the grill to reheat. From the refrigerator came a platter of lamb chops ready for broiling.

While the chops broiled the men quickly unfolded two card tables. These were readily set for eight, with plates, glasses, silver, baskets of crusty French bread cut from a long loaf and decanters of claret.

The chops, broiled over hickory embers, were delicious. So was the macaroni. These were followed by a mixed green salad in two big wooden bowls, served on wooden plates (the result of clever buying), and with a wooden tray of four superlative foreign cheeses. Then came coffee, which had perked aromatically during the first courses.

There was no doubt about it being a successful little evening from the sound of the first, welcoming cocktail to the last good-by. Everyone remembered afterward that Harvey had not said very much. But his eye kept going to Miss D—— the way a pearl diver's goes to a large lustrous pearl.

Miss D—— is now Mrs Harvey. The Harveys live in a comfortable but not too large apartment. They entertain a good deal at small, informal friendly parties. Mr Harvey is becoming quite famous as a host in his own peculiar way. His men friends take Mrs Harvey aside now and then to tell her that her husband is firmly convinced she is the most wonderful woman in the world. "He says you can give a dinner for eight and not raise a ripple."

# 5

# DINNER PARTIES

## And How They Grow

LET US SUPPOSE you have asked six people to dinner to meet the general manager of your husband's firm and his wife who are visiting your city.

Naturally you want everything to go off with a flourish and with a disarming air of ease. You want your husband's boss to increase his respect for your husband. And (being a woman) you wouldn't mind *too much* if the boss's wife were to say to her husband later: "No wonder Jones does so well for the company. You only have to see that clever wife of his . . ."

Your guests may not be old friends (they may be strangers to you until that evening); nonetheless, there's nothing stiff or formal about the welcome you give them.

In the living room the drinks are ready on their table for the host to serve them as the party gathers. These are ready to be served *at once* so there is no awkward standing around, waiting for the party to begin. Be sure to have a pitcher of well-chilled, savorily seasoned tomato juice for those who don't drink anything stronger. Lemon juice, celery salt, a dash of Worcestershire or A.I. sauce transform plain tomato juice into a delicious cocktail, especially if you have one of those little wooden pepper mills on the tray and top off each glass of tomato juice with a few grains of freshly ground black pepper.

It's ridiculous to go in for elaborate or many canapés before dinner, I think. Two kinds are really plenty. They are just appetizers to pique the appetite for the delicious dinner which is to follow.

## Table Decorations

DECORATING THE DINNER TABLE for any occasion is a direct challenge to your imagination. Especially today, when the old hard-and-fast rule of dead-white linen damask is threatened by any number of enchanting colored cloths of all sorts of materials.

Here are a few suggestions to start you off with and to thinking along your own lines:

1. A silver-gray cloth of silky-looking damask (actually rayon), used with silver candelabra, silver luster plates, clear glass and a low silver bowl filled with yellow mimosa, daffodils or California poppies.
2. A cloth of crepe de Chine, white ground sprinkled with bouquets of bright flowers. (Get the silk by the yard and make the cloth yourself, with a deep hem, hemstitched.) Use Dresden china with this. Or very pale green glass. Or opaque white glass candlesticks, vases and plates. Delphiniums or Chinese forget-me-nots for the centerpiece.
3. For a winter dinner party, when you want to be "gala," try the effect of a dark green damask cloth. (Perhaps you have some old damask curtains you could have dyed.) With this use gilt candelabra. (It

doesn't cost much to antique gild your old brass ones.) And a low ar-rangement of green and purple grapes in the center of the table.

4. A pale green tablecloth with all-white Wedgewood china, clear glass and a centerpiece of water lilies floating in a low glass bowl. Or magnolia blossoms.

5. A white damask cloth used with blue and white Canton china, clear glass and decorations of bright scarlet geraniums and delicate sprays of pearly white snowberries in a large blue-and-white Canton bowl.

6. A sky-blue cloth and napkins with a centerpiece of deep pink camellias. The china used with this might be like some I have recently designed. It has a broad band of glossy dark green, the color of camellia leaves, around the edge. And in the center of each plate a huge pink camellia.

7. A soft dusty-pink tablecloth (why not Tintex one of your old ones?) with a centerpiece of very dark red roses. Use red glass plates, goblets and candlesticks. You don't have to depend on heirlooms for this table decoration. You'll find the glass I mean in the ten-cent store.

8. And for a very hot summer night a white, silky damask cloth, with white-and-green glass plates, vases and candlesticks. And a centerpiece of maidenhair fern.

No matter what sort of tablecloth you decide on you should have a felt cover under it next to the table. This should come down on all sides to within a few inches of the floor and as far as the tablecloth comes. The felt cover not only protects the table, but its thickness greatly increases the handsome effect of your tablecloth.

## Be Original

THE TABLE doesn't necessarily need flowers. You can make a center decoration of handsome fruit (or even of well-scrubbed vegetables). Shells can make very effective table decorations. So do little china figures, either antique ones or those made by the modern designers. In England one sees frequently a beautiful old covered dish—of silver or some fine china. Why not get out Grandmother's old soup tureen and try it on your table the next time you have friends to dine with you?

Build up a store of interesting table decorations that you can use from time to time for special occasions. Jumble Sales, thrift shops and auctions often bring odd and beautiful things to light. If you own some lovely things *put them to work.*

The value of the centerpiece is to provide a center of interest which serves to draw everyone at the table together. But do keep it low enough so no one has to peer over or around it to see who else is at the table.

But the center of the table is not all the decoration. There are the candles at dinner. Colored candles are never as decorative as white ones. Except at Christmas, when I use red. Don't use candle shades, because the living flame of the candle is much too beautiful and has too much sentiment and romance connected with it in everyone's mind to hide it with anything. There are hurricane lamps, with tall shades of clear glass, which are lovely on a table or used to light the sideboard. I have seen some made to hold flowers around the base so the light comes up out of a mass of blossoms.

## Setting the Table

SEE THAT EVERY BIT of silver on your table is as bright as vigorous polishing can make it. Be strict about this. Even to the point of having an expert silver polisher come in and clean it for your party if necessary.

Every piece of glass should gleam brilliantly. (Hot water and soapsuds will attend to this.)

Dinner at eight

At each place is a service plate. This need not be larger than a conventional dinner plate. In fact, why not use dinner plates? The service plates should be part of the color scheme of the table setting. If you own some very handsome ones you may want to build your table decoration around them to show them off. If you don't, use dinner plates to match the ones you intend using for the courses which are to come.

You can use the same china for all the courses. Or vary this from course to course, always keeping your original color scheme in mind, of course.

Dinner napkins should be *large*, at least twenty-four by twenty-four inches. The embroidered monogram on a damask napkin of this size should be at least two inches high—larger, if possible. Remember that size in these details always makes for smartness.

Of course all the flat silver which will be required for all courses is arranged beside the service plate. And glasses for water and for wine.

There is no food on the table except a soft roll at each place (hard rolls mean crumbs). And the little silver or glass dishes of candies and salted nuts. Cigarettes, matches and an ash tray are set between every two places.

If you want to use place cards see that the guest's name is written *plainly*. Perfectly plain heavy white cards with a narrow gilt border (you can buy them by the hundred at any good stationer's) make the nicest place cards, and they go with every sort of color scheme. (If you want to be very grand you can have your monogram or crest embossed on the cards.)

## Seating the Guests

IN MOST HOUSES the host and hostess sit at opposite ends of the table. At a long narrow table this arrangement works out better than when the host sits in the middle of one side and the hostess faces him. It lets them look out for all the guests and keeps the conversation moving around the table.

But here, too, there is no set rule. When I lunched at the White House recently lunch was served in the Little Dining Room, which has a long narrow table of the Duncan Phyfe type. The President sat in the middle of one side of this, and Mrs Roosevelt sat across from him in the middle of the other long side.

In seating your guests why not follow the European custom and pay no attention to age? Let the judge have the fun of talking to the debutante. And give the college boy a woman of forty as a partner.

If one of your guests is apt to be shy and silent give him a partner who can be relied on to put him at his ease at once and draw him out. Don't condemn any man (even your own husband) to sit between two chatterers. If it's a very long table try to put a woman who is lively and vivacious halfway down it. She will keep things going around her, while you hold up your end and your husband entertains those around him.

## Food

GIVING A DINNER PARTY isn't the effortful thing it was before we all began to count calories. Today five courses—soup, fish, meat with vegetables, salad and dessert—are considered a lengthy menu. Four courses—which may consist of a soup, an entree with vegetables, poultry or game with salad and dessert are preferable.

If you have a natural flair for planning delicious meals, and use some ingenuity, you can do it in three courses and give your guests all they want to eat and with still less bother and fuss.

Here again we come back to the point we have stressed before. Each dish should be perfect of its kind. It should be served *piping hot* or *icy cold*. There must be plenty of it. And it should be *presented attractively*.

The secret of all good cooking can be written: *flavor first*. Buy only first-class food. Again, this does not mean the most expensive cuts of meat or out-of-season fruits, vegetables or fish. One of the most delicious dishes I ever tasted was a goulash made of a cheap cut of beef but glorified with chicken livers, mushrooms, a rich brown sauce and seasoned with genius.

Foods which are in season are always the best flavored. Fresh cod or halibut, only a few hours out of the sea, are preferable to cold-storage lobster any time (and to every palate). Train your cook (if you have one; otherwise learn to do this yourself) to cook meats, fish and vegetables to keep their natural flavors.

If you want to add something quite different do this with a really good (and, alas! this means *rich*) sauce. *Beurre anchois*, for instance, which does something unforgettable to plain broiled halibut or cod. (Cream together unsalted butter and anchovy paste and spread this on the hot fish just before serving it.)

Why not learn at least three or four fine sauces and how to make these down to perfection? The three might be hollandaise (to be used on fish and on certain vegetables); béchamel (a very rich white sauce); and béarnaise (delicious on beef); or Newburg sauce. You may want one sweet sauce for puddings. Perhaps a wine sauce. Study one or two of the best cookbooks (you'll find several of these listed in the bibliography at the end of this book) and practice on the family until you are skilled. Try a béarnaise sauce on hamburgers!

Exercise your ingenuity (and pore over your cookbooks) to plan a menu which will mean the very least amount of work in the kitchen at the last moment. Of course if you're determined to have a soufflé (which *has* to be eaten the very minute it is taken from the oven) you can manage one if everything else at the meal is something which can be cooked that morning or even the day before.

Here are several dinner menus I worked out some years ago which are practical in a small house, either to prepare yourself or with the help of only one maid.

1. Black-bean soup. (Canned, of course. But doctored just before serving with sherry, lemon juice and a thin slice of lemon sprinkled with paprika on each plateful.) Curried shrimp, served in a ring of boiled rice. The curry sauce is made well ahead of mealtime (curry gains flavor by standing). It is kept hot in a double boiler; the shrimps are added just at dinnertime while the rice is steaming. Cold roast turkey (roasted the day before) and a mixed green or a vegetable salad. A melon mold of ice cream ordered from the confectioner's. Or loose from the corner drugstore, packed in your own melon mold and hardened in ice and salt.

2. Half a cantaloupe filled with cold jellied madrilene. Hot Hungarian goulash with rice or *gnocchi.* A mixed vegetable salad—string beans and tomato jelly or chopped beets and water cress. Frozen rice pudding with fresh raspberries. Or peaches and cream with sponge cake, angel cake or really soft macaroons. Or warm fresh gingerbread.

3. Hot green-turtle soup (out of a can, with sherry added when ready to serve). Hot cheese soufflé or fondue. Cold chicken or turkey or cold baked ham with salad of *escarrole*, hearts of artichoke, celery and water cress and French dressing with a suspicion of garlic. Hot deep-dish berry or apple pie with lots of rich yellow cream to pour over it.

4. French onion soup, served in a big tureen at table into brown pottery bowls, with thin slices of toast floating in the soup and plenty of fresh-grated, *real* Parmesan cheese to sprinkle on. Finnan haddie creamed

with mushrooms in a rich sauce flavored with sherry and lemon juice. Steamed wild rice. Beet and water-cress salad with French dressing. Icy cold yoghurt with fresh raspberries. Or stewed green gages with hot gingerbread.

Let's go back over these dinner menus and analyze them. Each one has at least one hot and hearty dish. Only the cheese soufflé could be hurt by being required to stand for a late guest. And you can change this to cheese croquettes if you like, and forget the clock.

All are flavorful. The goulash is made of an inexpensive cut of beef but enriched with chicken livers, mushrooms, herbs and cooking sherry in the sauce.

All are colorful. The pale-colored finnan haddie and rice are companioned by the bright red beet salad. The dark black-bean soup and the goulash are followed by colorful courses which please the eye as well as tempt appetite.

## And Drink

GONE ARE THE DAYS when chablis was served with the oysters, moselle with the soup, burgundy with the roast, followed by champagne with the dessert. Today most people are content with one wine served throughout the meal (and very glad to get even that). This can be any one of the white wines (not too sweet). Or any of the red wines.

People talk a lot about wines, but my own private opinion is that practically no one, in America at least, knows a great deal about them. Our native wines are so good that you don't need to worry about foreign labels and vintage years.

Here's a tip I've discovered about serving wine:

When you serve a red California wine choose quite a heavy one. Burgundy, for example. Your guests, even the avowed connoisseurs among them, will taste this respectfully. And it seems a lot stronger than one of the lighter wines.

Start serving the wine immediately after the soup course. Why not get a real wicker wine-bottle basket to hold the bottle as it is passed? All the white wines require to be iced. If you serve red wine—bordeaux, chianti or burgundy—you might have the wine in decanters on the table. The guests can help themselves, and the tall glass decanters filled with ruby-colored wine are effective as part of your table decoration.

## Service

THE SERVICE about the table should be deft, quick and with no confusion about changing plates or passing the food. This is another reason for making the menu as simple as possible.

If you have just the one maid why have her in the dining room at all?

I once lived in a city house that had a basement kitchen with a dumb-waiter that came up into a pantry off the dining room. That winter when I had dinner parties I often had eighteen or twenty at one table; the first course was always on the table before we went in to dinner. Meanwhile the maid down in the kitchen placed the second course and the plates for it on the dumb-waiter and sent this up to the pantry. The men guests got up, took the used plates out to the dumb-waiter and brought in the next course. Everything went smoothly and very gaily. There were no dirty dishes in the pantry, and the maid was not asked to do more than she could do well.

It used to be the rule to serve the hostess first at table. Nowadays this has been superseded by serving the woman seated at the host's right hand (presumably she is the guest of honor) first of all. Next the servant goes to the host and so on around the table. The food, of course, is always offered at the person's left hand.

The finger bowls can be on the dessert plates (with a tiny fine-linen-and-lace doily under the bowl to keep it from rattling on the plate) when these are placed before each person at table.

Or if you are having an extra course of fruit after the dessert the finger bowls can be placed on the fruit plates.

When the time comes for after-dinner coffee it's entirely a matter of personal choice and convenience whether to have this at the table or in the living room.

If you decide on the latter catch your husband's eye when you think the time has come to make the move. Then get up and go. *At once.* Don't linger for the talk and gaiety to die down. Carry the party on into the living room on the tide of its own fun.

To come back to the question of coffee. If you aren't sure of your guests' preferences have two identical silver coffeepots (my own preference is for a Queen Anne or a simple modern pattern)—serve Sanka in one and strong coffee in the other.

## To Wait or Not to Wait?

THAT IS ALWAYS the question. Personally, I never hold up a meal for more than half an hour for *anyone*. It doesn't seem fair to the other guests who have made the effort (and often enough it *is* an effort) to get there on time.

If you wait too long the cook's temper will be spoiled (along with the soufflé). And no wonder.

Too, it's waiting about for late guests and for dinner that is answerable, I believe, for most of the overdrinking that happens at parties and which is stupid and boring. Everyone knows that it's the drinks taken *before* the meal that start the trouble.

## What Is Formal Entertaining?

EVERYBODY asks that question. Nobody knows the answer. My own feeling (and in this matter feeling is all anyone has to go on) is that the formality applies to the clothes you wear and the *perfection of every detail of the service* and not to anyone's behavior.

All social life today is freer and more fun than it used to be. The whole trend of modern life is toward more and more informal ways of doing everything. Who, today, wants to give up an evening to a stiff, pokey party?

Women, I venture to say, will always wear full décolleté on certain special occasions. Simply because this style of dressing can be so devastatingly becoming. I can't imagine any woman to whom nature (and the right sort of exercise and diet) has given a beautiful back and shoulders not wanting to wear the sort of dress which will show these off to perfection whenever she has a chance to do so.

But is there a single American husband who doesn't squirm at mention of a white tie and tails? It's not likely that you'll be able to persuade your husband into these clothes, not even though you do tell him how becoming they are to him. (They are to all men who are even halfway good-looking.) He won't believe you. He'll just mutter something about a dinner coat being more comfortable, and he'll turn up in one with a black tie.

And so will all the other men at the party, if given half a chance.

## CASE HISTORY OF A LADY WHO THOUGHT FORMALITY MEANT FUSS

All her life young Mrs Alison had been terribly keen about outdoor sports and terribly shy about indoor ones like dancing and formal dinner parties. She was happiest in riding clothes or in slacks and a sweater. They had to be superlative slacks, perfectly tailored (Mrs Alison was fastidious), but as for long swishy skirts and feminine frills, these gave her a bad case of the jitters.

She and Mr Alison lived on a ranch in Montana until Mr Alison got terribly interested in state politics and then in national ones and their friends and neighbors decided to send him to represent them in Congress.

All at once Mrs Alison saw stretching ahead of her a life in which she would be going to formal parties with a lot of people she didn't know and who, she felt, couldn't possibly care for *her*.

It wasn't that she disliked people. On the contrary, if she could have whisked them all out to the ranch and turned them loose to amuse themselves there she would have been completely happy. But she knew if she had to devote a good part of her life to going to and presiding over formal dinners she would rather divorce Mr Alison right then and there and die of a broken heart.

This was her state of mind when they started for Washington.

"Better get some evening dresses and fixings," Mr Alison said casually. "We'll probably have a lot of invitations right away."

"There," she thought miserably, "it's beginning."

The first invitation was to a dinner. The guest of honor was a minister from South America. Mrs Alison wore one of her new and lovely dresses and felt suddenly awkward and shy. But the look in Mr Alison's eye when he saw her was a great comfort.

The dinner party was at a house in Georgetown on a hot June night. It was a stately colonial house which might have seemed prim but for the roses and syringas that grew about the doorway and the lights streaming from the windows.

The door was opened by a gray-haired old colored butler, whose dignified manner somehow conveyed a sense of welcome as well. Within the long formal drawing room the light of many glowing candles played on old portraits on the white paneled walls. Through the windows could be seen the lovely evergreen garden.

When dinner was announced the stately procession of twenty-four guests led by the host with the wife of the ambassador on his arm, moved into the dining room. The long table—covered with snowy-white linen damask with tall shining silver candelabra and big silver bowls of yellow roses—was brilliantly lighted, though the rest of the room was filled with mysterious shadow.

Mrs Alison found herself between a senator and an archaeologist who had just returned from Crete. The senator immediately wanted to know all the details of ranch life. And Mrs Alison found herself wanting to ask a hundred questions about Crete, where she'd always wanted to go.

Dinner consisted of just four courses. But what delicious ones! Very hot clear green-turtle soup flavored with sherry. Perfectly deviled crabs. Spring lamb and green vegetables. And a deep-dish gooseberry pie with clotted cream to pour·over it.

Everyone talked gaily, delightfully, though (as Mrs Alison discovered to her amazement) most of those present had been strangers to each other until that evening. After dinner·the talk continued in the drawing room. She had a real sense of regret when it was time to go home.

That evening has persuaded Mrs Alison that she will not have to divorce her husband to escape a life with formal entertaining in it. She made the illuminating discovery that formality does not mean boredom and pomposity but grace and perfection of every detail. There was a challenge in that. Mrs Alison was too good a sport not to enjoy it. Today young Mrs Alison is spoken of as a great help to her husband who is now a figure in Washington politics.

# 6

# FAMILY GATHERINGS

## How to Enjoy Your In-Laws

**N**OT ALL THE OCCASIONS which cry out for a party depend on the calendar or on inviting guests outside the family circle.

There's the night your son gets home from his freshman year at college. There's the day thirteen-year-old Jane wins the essay contest at her school. There's the occasion when your husband returns from a week's fishing trip with a prize salmon, laid on ice and fresh ferns in a special wicker basket.

Times like these simply demand a celebration.

Now (I'm taking for granted that you've followed some of the suggestions in the earlier chapters) is the moment to look over your supply of table decorations. Choose something appropriate to the occasion. Dash out to the nearest ten-cent store and get some amusing favors, one for each person. A wooden soldier which is really a case full of pencils for literary Jane. A roll-up tape measure for the fisherman to measure his prize.

You may be one of the lucky ones who have the gift of making rhymes and limericks to fit occasions like these. Then you can find time to scribble off a few lines to point the joke of each favor even while you're beating up eggs or stirring batter. All families adore family jokes. They never seem to grow too old not to be repeated again and again. Your family will think your verses amusing and clever even if *you* (and they) know that they limp a little here and there. I've never been able to make any rhymes myself. But I always appreciate those that other members of the family write.

## Home-Comings

PERHAPS YOU AND YOUR HUSBAND have been off on a winter cruise. For ten deliciously lazy, sun-filled days you have been living a carefree existence. Without the necessity to discuss the monthly bills or the state of the plumbing or the children's school report you and your partner in this absorbing game called marriage have discovered a lot of brand-new interests and stimulating topics for conversation.

In a sense you have discovered each other all over again.

Perhaps this makes you dread a little having the ship come back to its home port. It isn't that you don't love your house and your children and the life you have with them. It's just that you're a wee bit afraid that going back to them will cause you to lose this dear, delightful companion you've had during the holiday.

Suppose you knew that you were coming home to a party? Suppose, before the ship docked, the steward brought you a radiogram from a friend which read something like this:

WELCOME HOME YOU AND PETE DINING WITH US TONIGHT LOVE
EMILY

Then, suppose, when you got home and had hugged and kissed the children and seen them tucked into bed or on the way to it, you and your entertaining cruise companion started off to Emily's. Suppose there you found her and a number of your other friends eager to welcome you and tell you how glad they are to have you home again. Suppose you find them all anxious to hear all about your adventures. Wouldn't that convince you (if you ever had any doubt of it) that you have the nicest friends in the world? And that you wouldn't live anywhere else on earth than right where you *do* live?

"But," you say, "I'm not going on a cruise. Or anywhere." Perhaps not. Not right away. (If you study the statistics of the numbers of people who do go on cruises and consult the law of averages you'll realize that you *may* go any day.) However, one of your friends and her husband are sure to be going. And *you* can play the Emily role and give them a homecoming party when they return.

Most families have a celebration of some sort while the children of the family are home from school or college during the holidays. Often there are people outside the intimate family circle who would love to be asked to these parties. There's the nurse who took care of the children when they were little or very ill at some time. There's the family doctor who saw them through measles and green-apple stomach ache. He might find it fun to drop in on the party.

Every family has some relations who don't receive many invitations who frequently are lonely and feel neglected. They would enjoy seeing the young people play games and dance. Perhaps there's a cousin who is good at palmistry or reading handwriting. If so the young people will flock around her. And she, being human (even if she is a relation or even an in-law), will adore displaying her specialty.

We Americans are more age-conscious than Europeans usually are. We tend to separate people into groups according to years. I think this is a pity. It limits the horizon for young and old. When you go to a party anywhere in Europe you find young and old and middle-aged people all having fun together. In this way young people learn to feel at ease with their elders and older people are never stiff or at a loss for conversation with their children's friends.

A woman I know who has visited a great deal in the great houses of England and Scotland told me that one of the bright spots of her life was a big family party in a country house near Edinburgh, when she saw a dignified old dowager duchess park her tiara on the mantelpiece to dance a Highland fling with her *fourteen-year-old great-grandson!*

## Birthdays

BEING INESCAPABLE, birthdays should be taken gaily. If it's your own birthday that is hovering on the horizon don't set your mind (and your lips) that you won't let anyone into the secret (though I'm not one to want to know everyone's age or tell my own). Or that you won't let anything happen to prevent your meeting it as grimly as you now feel like doing.

Resist that impulse (though I know how difficult this is). It's that sly

Will to Be Dreary trying to make himself felt again. (He gets terribly determined around birthdays.) Put him down at once. And firmly. When a friend rings you up and asks you if you'd be free on the seventeenth to do something with her reply: "I don't know about the seventeenth. It's my birthday." She'll probably come back with: "Oh, is it? Then *of course* you and Pete must come to dinner (or to spend the evening) with us."

And you may be sure she is having fun dashing around getting pink candles and birthday favors, making a special birthday cake or ordering one from the Woman's Exchange, all in your honor.

When *her* birthday comes round you can have the fun of giving her a party.

No matter what the state of the world, your heart, or your finances it's not at all likely that you will let one of your children's birthdays go by without a special festivity to mark the day. This may be an all-day picnic at a lake with frankfurters roasted over a charcoal grill, or hamburgers.

If your family is picnic-minded why not get a stock of those metal, long-handled hamburger broilers? They cost about fifteen cents apiece. There's a metal form that holds the hamburger so that you can broil it over the open fire without danger of dropping it into the blaze. And the handle is long enough that you don't have to broil yourself too.

Perhaps the ideal birthday party is a clambake on the beach—clams and corn and sweet potatoes, steamed in fragrant seaweed over a bed of red-hot embers and stones. All these cook slowly and perfectly while everyone goes for a swim. Take along one or two chickens, split and cut in quarters and wrapped in Patapar paper. Or sew them in clean cheesecloth. Stow these away in the mass of seaweed to steam with the rest of the bake.

And of course the perfect dessert for such an outdoor party is ripe, chilled watermelon.

The time when birthday parties are most important is when the children are at the self-conscious, growing-up age. Just when some people might say they are too old for such nonsense. It's my belief that most of us are never too old for nonsense. And it's just when we may seem to be so that we're most in need of it and get the most good from it.

Why not use your camera to take pictures of the family on birthdays? And on other days too? One woman did this. She made a special Kodak book for each one of her four children. Each book was a complete record of the child's life—pictures of sports, holiday trips, Christmases and birthdays. One of the children is now an engineer out in China. His Kodak book is his most prized possession. Whenever he has a birthday in some remote part of the world he gets it out and recalls the family parties that were such fun. It keeps him from feeling too lonely.

I have a friend whose birthday and her husband's fall on the same day. They have a party on that day every year that all their friends look forward to.

Even if your husband's birthday doesn't come with your own don't let it pass without a celebration. What if he does protest at first? His shyness is probably just an attempt to cover up a real and natural eagerness to have a party of his very own.

Ask his friends. (Of course we hope they are yours too.) But the ones among your mutual friends that he likes best. Serve the kind of dinner he enjoys. Perhaps this is corned beef and cabbage. No matter. Remember, *all* good food that people like to eat is party food. And you can do something really magical to plain boiled corned beef with a hollandaise sauce to which you have added several tablespoonfuls of freshly grated raw horse-radish root.

Decorate the table with a big colorful bowl of fruit or vegetables piled on a flat wooden tray. Or you could arrange pots of scarlet geraniums and pots of trailing English ivy. Use a red-and-white-checked tablecloth with napkins to match. Or perhaps a dark blue linen cloth with red linen napkins.

Stunts always go well at a birthday party. And nearly everyone has a pet one he or she can do. Even if it's just balancing a glass filled with water on his forehead and, holding a lighted candle in each hand, lying down on the floor and getting up again. This is my only stunt, and I'm terribly proud of it.

Call for these when the birthday cake has been wished on and cut and the toasts are being drunk.

(You can learn a brand-new one yourself as a birthday surprise and to keep the ball rolling.) Often very quiet, apparently shy people have a pet stunt they do well (and love to do) or some skill like reading character from handwriting. Things like these always make a party go.

## Thanksgiving Day

DOES THE TURKEY make Thanksgiving? Or is it Thanksgiving that gives reason for the family dinner? If you believe the latter you will feel, as I do, that the oldest American holiday ought to mean a great deal more than two helpings of roast turkey, pumpkin pie and an uncomfortable, overstuffed feeling all the rest of the day and the next.

Thanksgiving is, above all else, a family day. A day when the four generations come together. It is the day on which to retell the old family stories—how Great-Grandmother L—— made the trip down the Ohio River on a flatboat when her parents started West with the pioneers. How Great-Uncle James ran away from home to go to sea and later sailed round the Horn to California. How Cousin William took up farm land and built a sod house to live in where there's a thriving industrial city today. Every American family has stories like these to remember. Part of the entertainment plans for Thanksgiving Day can be given to making time and a place for storytelling. During the family dinner or in the evening around the open fire, with a big jug of country cider and a bowl of fruit, nuts and raisins.

America's Thanksgiving Day dinner is a tradition. It would be a daring person, indeed, who would think of changing the historic menu of roast turkey and pumpkin pie. But there's no reason why this should mean stodginess.

A young uncle of mine and his wife who live in the country once invited all the family to spend Thanksgiving Day with them. Some came by train and some by automobile. It's a big family. When we arrived at this white Long Island farmhouse we found the front door flanked by two tall stacks of corn with golden pumpkins at the foot of each one. My uncle opened the door. He was dressed up like a farmer in overalls and a blue shirt and a wide straw hat. His wife was dressed like an old-fashioned farmer's wife in a prim pink calico dress and a starched apron and a sunbonnet.

The dinner table was stretched to its furthest capacity, and there was another table for the small children. Both tables were covered with cloths of big green-and-white-checked gingham (three-inch squares). My aunt had bought the gingham by the yard and hemmed the cloths and napkins to match. Down each table was a lovely arrangement of red apples, ears of corn, vegetables and fruits. On each table, too, were big old-fashioned jugs of beer and cider.

There were place cards with red turkeys on them. And shiny new tin plates from the ten-cent store. The first course was oyster soup, served in yellow bowls (also from the crockery counter of the ten-cent store). Then came the turkey (three of them, in fact, stuffed with creamed purée of chestnuts. I've said it was a large family). There were candied sweet potatoes and celery and a green vegetable. There was corn bread, sweet and piping hot. There was a mixed green salad served in little individual wooden salad bowls. And for dessert pumpkin pie, of course, and "country coffee" in big cups.

Everyone sat a long time around the table telling the old family jokes and stories. Then my aunt gave the signal and we all went into the living room where there was a piano. There was music laid out on it, all old-fashioned songs that everyone knew and could sing. Later on we had a magic-lantern show. The slides were photographs of members of the family when they were babies, and we had to guess who was who.

## Christmas

YOU DON'T NEED ME to tell you that to hang a really big wreath of evergreens tied with a smashing red bow on your brass door knocker will do something magical and Christmasy to everyone who goes past your house.

Or that a pair of little evergreen trees in pots, sprinkled with artificial snow, set on either side of your front door are as heart-warming as a Christmas greeting.

Or that a huge Christmas tree, hung with tinsel and blue and silver balls and lighted by dozens of tiny wax candles, performs a miracle for grownups as well as for children.

Like Thanksgiving, Christmas is a time for the family first of all. And for old friends. And for any new friends who you may happen to know are lonely or sad and who need exactly what you have to offer them in the way of Christmas fun, warmth and good cheer.

Trimming the house for Christmas, from getting the greens in the woods or buying them in the market to putting up the last spray of mistletoe where it will do the most good, is fun. The children adore these preparations. You can make this a party for them, in true Christmas style, if you have a winter picnic in the woods when you go after the greens. Build a fire. The scout in the family will know how to do this, even if the ground is covered with snow. Hang a pot over it, gypsy fashion, to heat the canned soup you have taken along. (Don't forget the can opener.) This with crackers, hamburgers broiled over the blaze, a square of gingerbread and an apple apiece make a perfect picnic meal.

If you go greens-gathering in the car hunt around for a huge gnarled yule log, to be wreathed with ground pine and brought in with ceremony for the fire on Christmas Eve.

And don't forget to brush away the snow from under the hemlocks to hunt for the bright red partridge berries to add color to your table center-piece. I've never had such a Christmas myself, but some day I hope to.

When it comes to decorating the table for the Christmas dinner you can let your imagination go. Have a red or silver or deep blue tablecloth.

Get it big enough to hang down to the floor on all sides of the table, and trim the sides with big loops of wide cellophane ribbon—silver on the blue or the red cloth; red on silver. Use red glass plates and glasses. And red candles. And mass the center of the table with holly.

Or you could make a crèche for the center of the table, using the tiny carved and painted wooden figures made by the European peasants. Group the animals around the figures of the Virgin and Christ Child, the Three Wise Men, the shepherds and angels. And then encircle the group with a delicate wreath of pine, holly and eerie mistletoe.

Or use a white damask cloth and have a small red-and-tinsel-decorated Christmas tree in the center of the table.

## My Christmas-Carol Party

THIS YEAR, about four weeks before Christmas, I shall send out the invitations to my twenty-second Christmas-carol party. Most of the friends I shall ask will be expecting the invitation, because most of them have been coming to these parties for nearly as many years as I have been having them.

All of them know exactly what the party will be like. The entertainment never varies, and all of them have a very real sentimental feeling for it.

This party begins in the afternoon, about five, when it is dusk and the candles on the Christmas tree will show at their loveliest. The tree, as tall a one as we can get into the living room, is at one end of the room, strung with strands of silver tinsel and hung with lots and lots of colored balls. Our dear old English nurse Frances Samson and I have hung trees together each year. For years I have been trying to decide which makes the loveliest effect—an all-silver tree with no color on it at all; a tree with some silver balls and some bright red ones; or a tree with blue and silver ornaments.

I think I've finally decided on the red, blue and silver tree as being the most effective against the walls of my living room.

There are no ornaments on the tree except the tinsel and the shining balls. And no presents. But there are dozens and dozens of tiny red, white and blue wax candles which we light when the party begins.

I happen to love real candles so much (surely you've guessed this by this time) that I risk the fire hazard. I have two pails filled with water behind the tree. And several brooms with big sponges fastened to them.

The friends who come to this Christmas party are of all ages. There are grandmothers, and there are tiny ones, so young they have to sit on someone's lap or be carried in someone's arms. And all the ages in between. They are my own and my mother's and my children's friends.

Before they come the long red curtains at the windows of the big living room have been drawn. The candles on the mantel and on the piano are lighted. There is no other light in the room except that from four softly shaded lamps and the gay, flickering firelight.

All around the room against the walls are big loops and swags of laurel rope caught up by *huge* festive bows of wide red-and-silver stiff paper. From some of the bows I hang three red paper Christmas bells, a big one flanked by two of smaller size.

When everyone has come several friends help me light the candles on the tree. Then everyone gathers around the piano, the tiny ones closest, and sing together the well-known old carols: "The First Noël" and "O Little Town of Bethlehem" and "I Saw Three Ships A-Sailing." One of my friends always plays for us. He says he looks forward to this as the part of the Christmas season he enjoys most of all. When I first started to have this party I got seventy-five little paper-covered books of carols which may be purchased from any music publisher. These are brought out year after year along with the tree ornaments.

After the carols my friend strikes up a lively march. I choose one of the little children and we lead the march into the dining room where the little ones have supper. This is always hot cereal and milk, creamed chicken, bread and butter, vanilla ice cream and sponge cake. The table is spread with a red-and-white paper cloth and trimmed with a small, gaily decorated Christmas tree, with Santa Clauses and red paper favors. There's a little inexpensive present for each child—a tin horn, a drum, a puzzle or an amusing painted wooden animal.

I have very little to do with this part of the party because the responsibility of the children's supper is taken off my hands by "Nannie." She comes to the party every year and wouldn't miss presiding over the children's supper for *anything*.

Meanwhile there are cocktails, tea and turkey sandwiches for the rest of us in the living room. Often that part of the party goes on with more singing and dancing. People don't seem to want to go home. And that, of course, means a party is a success.

This is my favorite party. I look forward to it from one December to the next. It has everything that I sincerely believe makes a party go—beauty of setting, warmth of welcome, good food and fun that everyone takes part in.

## HOW GREAT-GRANDMOTHER WENT TO BERMUDA

Mrs Oldcastle was a conservative. She clung to the past like a mussel to its rock. And to every piece of furniture, rug and picture she had put into her house when she and Mr Oldcastle furnished it the year Garfield was elected.

Mr Oldcastle had not liked change. And he believed in buying things that would last.

They had lasted. For one thing, the furniture had not had a great deal of use. The Oldcastles never gave any parties. The Oldcastle children quickly grew up, married and moved into homes of their own. When Mr Oldcastle died Mrs Oldcastle settled down into an existence which left everything in the house exactly as it had been in the days when Mr Oldcastle was expected home from the office every evening at exactly six o'clock.

Mrs Oldcastle really didn't like all these ways of doing things, but she believed that at sixty-five she was too old to change. Besides, she was a great-grandmother. That seemed to make any change in her established routine slightly improper.

Her children tried to jolt her out of this rut. Her eldest daughter, Gloria (who was herself a grandmother), wanted her mother to sweep out all the shiny mahogany cabinets and tables and all the brown over-stuffed chairs and sofas and have new, modern, light-colored furniture. Her second daughter, Doris, knew about psychology and things like that. "You'll get a neurosis or something if you live with nothing but memories," she prophesied. Mrs Oldcastle's son Jim was practical. "The thing for you to do is to move into a nice modern apartment," he said bluntly. "You'd be more comfortable and save money besides. You don't need half this space. You never have anybody stay with you, do you, except the girls once or twice a year and me when I come on from Chicago? And I can always go to a hotel."

He almost added aloud: "I'd be more comfortable there."

What her children said was perfectly true, but it disturbed Mrs Oldcastle nonetheless. She couldn't bring herself to do what Gloria and Doris suggested. And she was determined to stay on in her nice, comfortable big house which she could perfectly well afford to do. She decided she would show Jim that she *did* need all that space and she *would* entertain. Then it occurred to her that she had not entertained or gone to other people's parties in so many years that she hardly knew anyone to ask. Her life was completely bound up in her children and her grandchildren. That gave her an idea. There were five grandchildren at three different boarding schools. She wrote her children that she would like to have all the grandchildren spend a day and a night each with her during their Christmas vacations.

It wasn't a successful visit. The children arrived full of spirits. But somehow their cheerfulness began to wane before they had been in their grandmother's house an hour. They were polite. Too polite. But all too evidently bored. Conversation at dinner dragged. After dinner they fidgeted around the living room until Mrs Oldcastle became so nervous she forgot this visit was for *fun* and began to scold. In desperation she bundled them all off to a movie. (Most of them had already seen it.)

Next day after the children (still polite but even more bored) had left, Mrs Oldcastle went to bed with a raging headache and a bad cold. After coming every day for two weeks the doctor said to her: "I haven't a single pill that will do you any good. I prescribe a trip to Bermuda. Go on the next boat and stay six weeks."

If one of her children had said this to her Mrs Oldcastle would probably have retorted that she had not spent a single night out of her own house for fifteen years. And had no intention of doing so. But the doctor was a Man in Authority. She went, meek as a lamb.

It was nearly three months later when she came back. When the front door opened and she stepped into the hall she got the shock of her life. Not a thing in the house was changed from the day she left it, but all at once Mrs Oldcastle realized that she was actually seeing her own house for the first time.

And what she saw was *dreadful*.

Her eyes which had feasted on pink-walled houses looped with green vines, roses and purple-flowered bougainvillaea, and on white roofs against bright turquoise skies, shrank from the drab tan walls, the dull engravings and etchings, the mulberry carpet, the solid brown upholstery, the big solemn bookcases stuffed with sets of books no one ever opened.

Depression settled down over her happiness like a damp fog. Suddenly life seemed so hopeless. She felt so *old*.

Before that old Will to Be Dreary took her captive again she made a bolt for the telephone. She rang up a young woman she knew who was a decorator. She asked her to come over *at once*.

The next three weeks were the busiest Mrs Oldcastle ever spent. And she was happier than she had been in years. She was horrified (but excited) at her own daring when she saw the painter actually painting every inch of woodwork in the house white and the outside of the house deep pink, with white shutters and trim and a *white roof* and a shiny dark green front door. When she saw the paper hangers putting up an enchanting paper with gay blue-and-white stripes (five inches wide) in the front hall she smiled to herself. (How horrified Henry Oldcastle would have been.)

The drawing room (she had decided to have one) had flat white walls and a soft pink ceiling. The old dark upholstered furniture was slip covered in rough white material, with white fringe around all the seams. The floor was painted black with a new plain, white rug. Two of the bookcases were painted white and the insides lined with deep pinkish-red velveteen to tone in with the ceiling. In these Mrs Oldcastle arranged some pieces of valuable, beautiful old china she had had for years.

She sent three baskets of ornaments and old lamps to the local thrift shop, keeping only a group of old Staffordshire figures to go on the mantel against the big sheet mirror which covered the whole chimney breast. This made the room ever so much larger and lighter than it had ever seemed before.

She got new lamps, big ones of clear glass, with white silk shades lined with shell pink, and two huge glass vases which she immediately filled with Bermuda Easter lilies. (She could afford them, fortunately.)

None of Mrs Oldcastle's children now ever suggest that she give up her house and move into an apartment. They seem to like to come and stay with her quite often in "Bermuda," as the family call her house. The grandchildren come often for week ends. They write and ask if they may.

Mrs Oldcastle no longer talks anything except humorously about being a great-grandmother. She gives small dinner parties (with awfully good food) and asks friends in to play backgammon.

The neighbors are frightfully excited about all these changes. It is hard to know which has caused the most talk: Mrs Oldcastle painting her house pink with a white roof, or Mrs Oldcastle's having her hair bobbed and permanently waved into a froth of short snow-white curls, or the retired major who is a frequent guest at Mrs Oldcastle's dinner parties. (I hear he is now teaching Mrs Oldcastle to drive a car.)

# 7

# SPECIAL OCCASIONS

## High Spots in Your Life

A WEDDING IN THE FAMILY—your own, your sister's or your child's—is a very special sort of an occasion. For one thing, even in these practical times, a wedding gives you a perfectly good opportunity to be as sentimental as you like. It allows you to satisfy all your love of romance.

There were two young people so sophisticated and so emancipated they professed not to believe in all the ceremony surrounding marriage until they met, fell in love and became engaged.

But after that revolutionary process known as falling in love neither one was ever heard to voice such an opinion. For a few weeks they spoke of going down quietly to the City Hall some day and being married "legally but without any ceremony." Then they began looking at churches. "After all," he was heard to remark, "there *is* something about being married with a religious ceremony. I'm told a wedding doesn't *have* to be fussy."

I went to their wedding. It was in the chantry of a beautiful Gothic church. There were no guests except the immediate families and half a dozen very intimate friends. About fifteen people. There were no attendants. The bride and bridegroom came in together. The bride wore a navy-blue-and-white street dress with an adorable tiny hat of white hyacinths, draped in a white face veil. There were white lilies on the altar and candles. And there was a sweet-faced old clergyman to read the solemn words of the marriage service.

There were smiles and kisses and a few wet eyes in the vestibule after the brief ceremony. And then there was champagne and chicken sandwiches and a bride's cake in the flower-filled living room of a friend's apartment. And more kisses and toasts and laughter and good wishes.

In short, there was a wedding.

Weddings divide under four general headings:

There is the big wedding, in a church, with a big reception afterward.

There is the big church wedding, followed by a small reception to which only the families and intimate friends are asked.

There is the small wedding, in a church, to which only a few friends and the two families are asked, followed by a *big* reception which takes in everyone.

And there is the very small wedding and reception both held at the bride's home.

It's entirely a matter of personal choice. Which one you choose depends on the size of your house and of the church (if you plan to be married there) and on the amount of money you are willing to spend on a wedding. You also have to take into account the size of your family and his and the number of friends and relations you decide *must* be invited.

Suppose, let us say, that you live in an average-sized apartment in a city or a large suburb. It's ridiculous to think of getting all the friends you and your fiancé would like to ask into it for a wedding reception. But if the church you have chosen to be married in is large you can ask everyone to the ceremony and ask only the two families and a few very intimate friends to the house afterward.

Or if you live in a small town or in the country where churches are apt to be small and houses big and roomy you can reverse this arrangement. Perhaps you have a lovely tree-shaded lawn where the reception can be held. You could be married there under an elm tree. Or against a screen of vines on the porch of the house, while the guests stand about on the lawn.

A wedding such as this is a lovely one to remember all your life. And it need not cost a great deal. There is only the clergyman's fee (which the bridegroom pays), the food (and this can be as simple as you choose) and your own wedding dress and veil.

If you choose something very simple for this (say white dotted muslin) make the dress with a skintight bodice and a tremendously full skirt. Perhaps over a hoop even. Such a dress could be worn the rest of the summer. (And which I'm sure will be ravishingly becoming.)

You see the same principle applies here as in making a pair of curtains. Lots and lots of inexpensive material has much more effect than expensive material used skimpily.

If you have room for a big reception be sure to ask everybody. Don't leave out one of the old family friends. Or any of the people who knew you when you were a little girl. If you are going to engage some extra maids to help on the day of the wedding think if there is not some old one, who knew you when you were a child, who could be asked to do some small service (she could look out for people's coats perhaps) on that day. And who would adore to have the opportunity to be *in* the wedding.

## Wedding Decorations

BEING INTERESTED in beauty and how this is achieved, I simply can't help seeing all the details of a wedding in terms of decoration. The procession of bridesmaids up the aisle, the grouping of them during the ceremony and the arrangement of flowers and greens all make effects which should be lovely and romantic and youthful. And yet dignified.

The bridesmaids' dresses can be strikingly simple and of inexpensive materials. Crisp, colored organdy is lovely. But they *must* be all exactly alike to create the right effect. The bride's dress can be of lace or satin or of organdy or crossbarred dimity. But it and the attendant's dresses *must* conform in style. If your bridal gown is very, very full and flowing you don't want your bridesmaids to be tailored and streamlined.

The same basic rules which apply to decorating the house apply equally to decorating the church or the room in the house where the wedding is to take place.

Of course you want flowers and greens, lots and lots of them. You can make a lovely effect using big sprays of white flowered dogwood which form a background for lilacs or peonies or lilies or roses. The flowers used should be all of one color. And just one kind of flower is usually more effective than several kinds. Arrange them in big masses for effect. Balance these masses. Remember you are creating an architectural setting.

Remove all the small objects and pictures from the room, leaving only the flowers for decoration.

And in choosing your flowers have a thought for the color of your curtains. Take these down if they are not going to contribute to the color effect of the room. Or get some brand-new inexpensive ones that will strike the same note as the floral decorations.

## A City Wedding

THE BRIDE had chosen to be married in one of New York's old and rather dark churches. The darkness was lighted by many, many white Easter lilies which led your eye up the aisle to the chancel. There there were more lilies against masses of ferns and dark rhododendron leaves massed around the candlelit altar.

The very tall young bride was like a lily herself in her long-skirted Empire satin gown. It had been her mother's wedding dress. There were no bridesmaids. Instead she was preceded up the aisle by three little girls. They wore long-skirted Kate Greenaway dresses of pale green chiffon velvet, with red ballet slippers and red sashes. On their dark hair were wreaths of huge real red tulips. And they carried great bouquets of red tulips as well.

## In a New England Village

THIS IS A WEDDING PICTURE I brought back from one of those old towns in Massachusetts where flocks of white-painted houses gather around an elm-shaded village green. The bride's family has lived in one of those houses since pre-Revolutionary days.

The wedding was held in the old white church at one end of the green. The high-backed pews were filled with relations and friends, many of whom had come from various places by train. The windows and doors stood open, so that the music and the words of the wedding service could be heard by lots of other friends who stood outside on the green.

The bride's dress was of very, very full white organdy. Her veil was of floating tulle. Her large bouquet was made of big petaled white daisies. The bridegroom and best man were in white flannels with dark blue coats.

After the ceremony bride and groom walked down the aisle, down the church steps, along the elm-shaded village street and home, with all the wedding guests following after them.

There was a buffet table set out on the lawn under the old gnarled apple trees and lots of little tables and movable chairs. There was no caterer. The very simple "breakfast" had been cooked and prepared in the house and in the kitchens of friends. Other people in the town came in themselves to help serve this or "lent" their maids.

I remember that all the furniture had been moved out of the living room to make a space for dancing. The local fiddler had been engaged to stand on the porch outside and play old-fashioned tunes for young and old to dance luck to the wedding.

When I remember this wedding and compare it with some of the big, noisy weddings held in country clubs or hotels it seems incredible that anyone who could possibly manage the former would choose the other kind.

# AFTERNOON TEA AT HOME
## The Time for Your Friends

THE PROBLEM  To arrange the tea table in the living room without disarranging the room and to create a center for leisurely conversation.

THE SOLUTION  1. In this charming pine-paneled room in a New York house the large, low, square tea table is set in front of the sofa and before a blazing fire every afternoon during the winter. The usual arrangement of chairs and sofa provide places for four close to the table. Other light chairs can be quickly drawn up if there are more guests for tea.

2. A linen-and-lace cloth covers the table under the antique silver tea service. The hostess sits at one end of the sofa and pours the tea herself.

3. Plates of paper-thin bread and butter, hot biscuits and home-made cookies or toasted English muffins with honey or jam are placed on the tea table for the guests to help themselves. Though this is a large house and well staffed, no servants wait on the guests at tea after the tea service and food have been brought in.

# COUNTING THE INCHES
## In an Infinitesimal Apartment or in the Small House

THE PROBLEM   To get as much use as possible when entertaining out of a small entrance hall.

THE SOLUTION   1. The walls and woodwork of this small, square foyer in a New York apartment have been painted sky blue. The wall space between the front door and the door of the hall closet is fitted with a Servidor, also painted sky blue. This has sheet mirror at its back to give the illusion of a deeper space.

2. The shipshape shelves of the Servidor hold a carefully chosen stock of bottles and an assortment of glasses for all sorts of drinks, to be made at the triangular shelf which lifts up against the sheet mirror to form a workable bar.

3. The hall closet (behind the closed door) holds equipment for parties, bridge tables, games, half a dozen small folding chairs and a nest of little low tables useful for buffet suppers in the apartment's big living room.

4. It also holds, when not in use as here, the folding gadget for hats and a fold-up coat rack (not illustrated). The umbrella stand (a good one that fits neatly into a corner) is on duty all the time.

# EIGHT FOR SUPPER
## A Buffet Table That Combines Hospitality with Distinction

THE PROBLEM   To make service easy, keep food hot and create a picture your guests won't forget.

THE SOLUTION   1. The table itself is black lacquer—an effective background and one that doesn't mark—set against a mirror panel in which is reflected the flowered paper on the opposite wall.

2. Big silver candelabra hold *tall* candles that really illuminate. Napkins are heavy cream white with wide green borders. Two piles of lovely old plates are in various shades of *rouge de fer* with touches of blue on a cream-white ground.

3. The food is kept hot in earthenware baking dishes, which may also be used in the oven.

4. Cold turkey, on a silver platter, is surrounded by tomatoes and water cress. The carving knife and fork are of stainless steel.

5. The salad course is set on another table (not shown) which is later used for the service of dessert. Coffee may also be served here or in the living room.

# THE AFTER-DINNER SNACK
## Or When Friends Drop in During the Evening

THE PROBLEM   To place drinks and a bite to eat in the living room where your friends can help themselves easily.

THE SOLUTION   1. A black lacquer table with end leaves, admirably placed against a black wall and under a handsome modern water color, becomes a buffet at need.

2. The butler's tray is covered with green leather, studded with chromium nails and lined with chromium. This has been brought in from the kitchen with drinks, glasses and a vacuum pail for ice cubes.

3. The drinks offer something for all tastes: scotch, soda water, ginger ale, a tall pitcher of iced fruit juice and a jug of milk.

4. The snack consists of plain biscuits, a fine cheese and a basket of apples.

5. The tall candelabra with their lighted candles are decorative and add a festive touch.

# FIRST IMPRESSIONS
## Making Your Front Door Say "Merry Christmas"

THE PROBLEM   To welcome your guests the minute they get out of the car.

THE SOLUTION   1. A laurel wreath that is big enough and lovely enough to be more than a mere conventional gesture.

2. Posed against a door, lacquered a dark shiny green, as serenely weatherproof as it is smartly effective.

3. A big brass knocker, polished till you can see your face in it. A big door mat on which you can really stamp off the snow.

4. A black-and-white dog—yours may be gray or brown—to wag a welcome to his friends and yours, as only a nice dog can.

# THE MEAL OUTDOORS
## Informal and Yet Charming

THE PROBLEM   To create an atmosphere of casual hospitality that has just the right amount of order to keep it in balance.

THE SOLUTION   1. The table is of light wood, unpainted but scrubbed to a satiny paleness. The chairs, also light and unpainted, are covered with beige-colored leather. The effect is intentionally informal, but there is no lack of elegance.

2. Table and chairs are movable, to be placed in sun or shade, facing the pleasantest view.

3. The plates, linen and glass are Mexican. The Guadalupe Virgin bottle holds wine to be poured. The little figures, slumbering under their broad sombreros, are not only decorative but hold pepper and salt for the one-course meal which is to come.

4. There is nothing on the table that is not necessary to the meal itself except the flowers. But the effect is colorful, inviting and refreshing on a summer day.

# THE HOSTESS'S TREASURE CHEST
## Smart Things to Buy—or Hints for Next Christmas

THE PROBLEM  To gather together a collection of objects that lend distinction to various kinds of entertaining.

THE SOLUTION  1. On these glass shelves you'll see a miscellaneous assortment of the things every hostess wants, varying widely in price, to be picked up from time to time.

2. For drinks there are decanters for whisky and for sherry, a silver-plated vacuum ice pail, a chromium-plated cocktail shaker that never needs polishing.

3. For cigarettes there are good-looking ash trays—of which, of course, you'll need flocks. Both specimens are generous in size, one extra large to please men guests. There is also a crystal cigarette box.

4. Big crystal vases can hold flowers—or just green laurel leaves, than which nothing is smarter or less expensive. A leaf-shaped salad bowl from Honolulu makes even the simplest salad an event. The big metal bell may call week-enders to meals, to swim or to dress for dinner.

## Strictly without Fuss

THAT WAS HOW this young couple insisted they wanted to be married. Also, they did not want to have a religious ceremony. They wished to be married by a justice of the peace.

But both of them balked at the idea of having the only wedding either of them ever intended to have in a dingy office in the City Hall, with only a bored clerk to witness it.

What they finally did was this: They, with the bride's parents and the bridegroom's mother, went by train down to the bride's parents' place in the country. It was very early in April. The house was tightly shut up, with only a caretaker in it. (The young people had expected to be married there in the summer, but the young man suddenly landed a job several states away and they could not see the use of waiting.)

Perhaps you think a shut-up country house a dreary place to be married in. But it wasn't. The caretaker had built a big roaring fire in the huge fireplace in the hall. He cut and brought in armfuls of yellow-flowered forsythia and set these about in vases against the dark oak-paneled walls, until the hall seemed filled with spring sunshine. By arrangement the old white-haired justice of the peace had driven over in his Ford and was waiting there to marry the young couple in front of the blazing fire.

It was the very simplest sort of a wedding. Afterward there was some hot soup, chicken sandwiches and champagne. Certainly it was strictly without fuss. But it had dignity, sentiment and beauty of surroundings— all the essentials of a perfect wedding.

A wedding patterned after this is the easiest sort of a wedding to have. Even if your parents are dead, or if they live a thousand miles away, you are sure to know *someone*, a relation or a friend, who has a house in the country somewhere. This might be a bungalow perched on a hillside overlooking a glorious view, a cottage by the seashore or a farmhouse bowered in apple orchards. This friend will be only too thrilled at the idea of lending her house for a wedding. Who wouldn't be?

Or, if you didn't want to go out of town at all, there is sure to be a friend who would be overjoyed to fill her living room with flowers and have a minister or a magistrate marry you there. It seems to me that a couple loses something very precious if the memory of their wedding does not carry with it beauty of atmosphere.

## Anniversaries

WEDDINGS, in the natural order of events, mean anniversaries later on. One of the stock American jokes is about the husband who never remembers the anniversary of his own wedding and the wife whose feelings are hurt by this neglect.

But why wait for your husband to forget? Why let the day develop into a mood? Why not say blithely two or three days before: "The ninth is our anniversary. Don't you think it would be fun to ask Jane and Bill and the Warings and two or three more to come over that evening and have a party in the game room?"

Ten chances to one he'll reply: "Swell! Just what I've been thinking. You'd better order a case of beer, hadn't you? Or, wait a minute. After all, this is an *occasion*. Suppose I see about getting some champagne?"

And twenty chances to one the champagne will set him thinking in the right direction. *Your* direction. He'll call up the florist and send you some extra-special flowers. And (it's not at all unlikely) a present too.

P.S. You can use this formula regularly once a year, indefinitely. It's the one absolutely infallible answer to all the forgotten anniversary stories, plays and jokes.


## A Coming-Out Party That Was Fun

SEVERAL YEARS AGO a debutante I know was presented by her grandmother at an afternoon reception. This was really a glorified tea party at which the young girl was introduced formally to her grandmother's and mother's friends. She stood beside her grandmother and received the guests.

A day or so later her mother gave a party for the debutante and her own young friends. This was a dinner dance. About fifty young people were asked, and several of the mother's friends gave dinner parties for their young people on the same evening and brought them on to the debutante's dance afterward.

The party was held in the big living room. (It could be handled just as well, but not so charmingly, in a club.) At one end of the room they set up a real oyster bar with a special oyster man in immaculate white linen to open oysters from a barrel, as many as the young people could eat. The oyster man came from the fish market which supplied the oysters. At the other end of the room was a real grill and a chef in high white cap and apron who broiled delicious slices of juicy steak to order.

With the steak there were baked potatoes, split, buttered and reheated. And a green vegetable. Dessert was pumpkin pie and vanilla ice cream.

Small tables were set around the room, each one covered with gay paper tablecloths and napkins to match and candles in glass holders.

The center of the room was cleared for dancing, and the music for this was furnished by two extremely good Negro musicians.

There were a lot of more elaborate coming-out parties that year (some of them cost a very great deal), but this was the party these young people (now most of them married) still remember and talk about as being the most fun.

## Music for Dancing

MUSIC FOR DANCING should be good. And by "good" I mean *tops*. This doesn't mean that you have to engage a famous swing band or even a large orchestra. It *does* mean that one really good man at the piano is better than a wobbly orchestra of three or four pieces.

If you're having a dancing party whatever else you may decide to economize on *don't let it be the music.*

## Coming Out in the Country

NOWADAYS there's an increasing tendency among young people to have their coming-out parties in the country during the late summer or very early in the autumn before the colleges open.

If you are going to give such a party for your daughter then be sure to include with the invitations a little hand-drawn and printed map showing how to get to your house by motor. On the day of the party see that some illuminated signs are put up at any confusing crossroads where motorists could lose their way. Also engage three or four men from the local garage to wait by the front door and take the cars of guests who have driven themselves and drive these to the parking space. You wouldn't have to pay them more than a dollar or two each, and your guests will greatly appreciate the convenience.

I remember one lovely coming-out party last year in a big pink brick house set on a rise of scrubby wild land near Ipswich, Mass. When we turned in at the gate it was too late and too dark to see anything but the stars overhead and the lights streaming from the house ahead of us. But there was the fragrance of the millions of wild roses that scramble over the hillside and the fresh, biting tang of the far-off sea.

Our host was standing on the porch outside the open front door to welcome us—a picturesque figure in his pink Master-of-Foxhounds coat and black satin knee breeches. Inside, in the flower-decorated living room, stood his wife and their daughter, the debutante.

The house has a wide hall which runs straight through the middle of it to a grass terrace across the back. A floor for dancing had been laid over the grass and a red-and-white canvas tent roofed it over.

The party went on and on with loads of young people and older ones too. I remember the debutante's old nurse (she had brought up her mother also) seated in state where she could watch everything and see her child's fun and the young people she had known as small children coming up to talk to her.

Of course you may not have a huge pink brick house overlooking the sea or a husband who looks well in a pink coat (few of us have), but my reason for describing this particular party isn't the house or the pink coat. It's the *feel* of the welcome, the lights, the cordial greetings and the bringing together of as many as possible of those who have known and loved the debutante all her life. And no people asked just to make a crowd for effect or pay off social (or business) obligations.

Country coming-out parties usually go on all night. When dawn comes up there is a breakfast of scrambled eggs, little sausages or perhaps waffles with maple syrup and coffee. After which the guests pile into their cars, calling gay good-bys, and drive away home.

The debutante and her mother and father go to their beds tired but happy, knowing that the party has been a huge success.

## A Calendar of Your Own

WE'RE ALL CREATURES of habit. Even to the point of liking the same parties year after year. Perhaps you think your friends want something startlingly new and different when you ask them to your house. They don't. At least not all the time.

One family I know has made it a custom for more than two generations to give a big fancy-dress party for the children of the family and all their friends on a certain date every summer. The young people look forward to the K——'s party from year to year and plan their costumes for it long ahead of time. They have games with prizes and dancing. They have a fishpond grab bag, with funny little favors. And the parents come and look on at their children enjoying exactly the same fun they used to have. The K——'s always have a photographer there to photograph the children, and each child receives one. These photographs become a record.

A woman dramatist who lives in New York has had a special party every year on Christmas night for more than twenty years. Everyone she has ever known knows that on that evening she has open house. Men and women of the theater and of all the arts who happen to be in the city, perhaps lonely or without any family or friends, know that they are welcome. They know they will find Christmas greens garlanding the door and mantel, tall white candles glowing, laughter, warmth, good talk, music. And a big bowl of delicious (and potent) eggnog and a huge black and plummy fruitcake. This party has helped more than one sad-hearted person over a difficult day.

A woman who loves her garden and has a beautiful one, though she does all the work in it herself, gives a garden party regularly every year when the roses are in bloom. She asks everybody, old and young. There is a buffet set out under the arbor with hot and iced tea, fruit punch and claret cup. And plates of delicious, simple sandwiches and famous sponge cake. The guests help themselves. They wander, glass in hand, up and down the garden paths among the flowers. From somewhere, far off, comes the sound of deliciously gay Viennese waltzes played by a friend of the hostess as an undercurrent to the party.

## My Mother's and Father's Christmas Dinners

IN OUR OWN FAMILY CALENDAR a star marks the Christmas dinner parties that until last year my mother and father used to have regularly for all the members of our rather big family. These were occasions, and though they happened year after year while two generations were growing up and although the pattern varied scarcely at all there was not one of the eighteen or twenty of us, young and old, who used to gather at those times, who did not feel a glow of expectancy from the moment that we arrived at the front door with its evergreen wreath tied with a scarlet ribbon. And although each of us knew exactly what was to happen and many of us tired by the Christmas activities not one of us would have wanted a change.

They can never happen any more now that my father has gone, and one reason why I want to describe them in full detail is that my children may have a picture of these dinners as I remember them . . . and also because they seem to represent much of the beauty and quiet graciousness of American family life, which in a way is symbolic of what we have been talking about.

The evening began, as I have described, at the front door and with that delicious thrill which gave one a sense of anticipation for what was to come. Immediately the door would be opened by old Hunt, the butler.

Hunt had served my family off and on for more than fifty years. In later years he came only on special occasions, and it would not have been Christmas for any of us without him.

That, I believe, was a great part of the charm of those parties. There was Hunt year after year, remembering each one of us. There was Annie, the old waitress, with her black dress and white organdy apron and high fluted cap. There was the white colonial dining room with its mahogany furniture and red brocade curtains, the three Gilbert Stewart portraits on the walls and the old silver tankard which George Washington gave my great-grandfather, Oliver Wolcott—and there was my father, courtly and gracious and happy at his end of the table, seated under the portrait of his father. I can see him now, as dinner progressed, smiling down the length of the table at my mother.

Year after year there were the same dear old family friends and relations who always dined with us at Christmas—Cousin Laura Roosevelt and Nick—the Phil Thompsons, Aunt Katie and Ned, the Minturn Le-Roys, Mrs Kessler, Cousin George Gibbs, Jack and Cecile, my brother

Roger, Betty and Cynthia and my own three children Diana, George and Penelope. For such a long time the years never took anything away —they only brought new faces and young faces to the table.

The table itself, with the heavy white damask tablecloth which had belonged to my mother's grandmother and which had woven in it the design of her house on the Hudson—the tall rococo candelabras and the centerpiece, filled with grapes and fruit—the sprays of scarlet-berried holly and the reflection of the candlelight on the red Bohemian glass, all composed a lovely picture.

The dinner was exactly what the Christmas feast should be—far too much food, but everything delicious and in keeping with the Christmas tradition. Even the jokes and stories did not vary very much from year to year. Phil Thompson always proposed a toast which we drank to our one-eyed laundress, "Old Mrs Smith," who made the plum puddings, and how good they were with their lighted brandy sauce! And then my father, looking so adorable in his immaculate evening clothes, would rise and make a speech of welcome to us all. Meanwhile my beautiful mother at her end of the table would be nervously awaiting her turn to be called.

How simple it all was and how charming. After dinner there would be some little gift, nothing more than a tiny remembrance, for each of us, including whatever stranger there was among us. Then we often did some little family tricks in the drawing room, my brother a mind-reading stunt, someone else his favorite trick, and later, the small children would go off to bed and some of us would go on to a gay party elsewhere —with many Merry Christmases and good nights.

# 8

# SUCCESSFUL WEEK ENDS

## For Hostess and Guest

**A** WEEK-END PARTY can be the greatest fun in the world, for those who come to it and for you who give it. For one thing, it lasts long enough to have a number of moods to suit every temperament.

First of all, there's the thrill of arrival, of seeing your friends again and making them welcome to your house. And by "welcome" I mean WEL-COME. There should be no halfhearted enthusiasm about the greeting you give them.

Whenever I think of or see the word welcome I immediately think of a house I am often asked to on Long Island. Usually it is dark when I drive up to it. But the windows on either side of the door are brightly lighted the minute the car swings round the circle of drive, and before it even stops the front door of the house is flung open and host, hostess and several excited dogs come rushing out to greet me. With a welcome such as *that* there isn't the least doubt as to whether or not your hosts really wanted you to come. They give you the impression they have been counting the minutes till you arrive.

In that particular house there are no servants at all. The husband and wife divide the household duties between them, with the help of a part-time maid. The husband takes charge of the marketing and cooking. He is a really superlative cook who turns out a cheese soufflé to melt in your mouth. The wife is responsible for all the rest of the house. And quite marvelously too.

When you go there to stay over a week end you never for one moment feel the lack of service to make you comfortable. And what is even more wonderful, you are never conscious of any extended effort on the part of your host or hostess.

The host carries your bag upstairs to the guest room. The hostess links her arm in yours and goes upstairs with you, chatting eagerly all the while. Your room, when you reach it, is brightly lighted, full of lovely color. A little vase of flowers and a tiny clock are on the bedside table. With one or two new and interesting books that you've been wishing to read and hadn't got round to yet. The bed is soft and inviting, with two pillows (one hard and one soft), a perfect lamp for reading in bed, with a high-powered bulb, and a light, as well as a warm, blanket. Folded at the foot of the bed is a down-puff.

There is also a comfortable chair by the window where you can sit pleasantly when you want to spend some time upstairs all by yourself. And an ottoman to put your feet upon. A small desk is fitted with note paper, envelopes, two or three postcards, several stamps, ink and several new pens, pointed and stub.

In the closet are lots of dress hangers of uniform size and color. The bureau drawers are lined with fresh white paper. (There's a new *perfumed* paint which comes in lovely bright colors which you can use to paint the inside of bureau drawers. It imparts a flowerlike perfume to whatever is put into them.)

On the bureau is a good face powder, cotton cleaners, hairpins and a pincushion with various kinds of pins and two needles threaded, one with white cotton, one with black silk.

The room has a scrap basket.

While you're taking all this in and appreciating the thoughtfulness of the hospitality your hostess has opened your bag placed on a bag rack. Deftly she is putting away your things in the bureau drawers and in the closet. While you're still telling her the news of mutual friends she has drawn your bath in the adjoining bathroom.

There, already laid out for you, are lots of luxurious big towels, soap, bath salts and bath powder.

In a little sewing room upstairs there is an ironing board and an electric iron which the hostess uses for her own pressing and which you can use too if your clothes need it.

This, I admit, is rank luxury. But also, I insist, it is luxury which a guest appreciates. It is done so expertly that you never once have the feeling that you are causing your friend a lot of bother. Only you feel rested and refreshed and *welcomed and loved.*

And you go down to the cocktails your host has shaken up for you (remembering your favorite kind) and to the perfectly delectable, though simple, dinner he has cooked, feeling gay and delighted and prepared to be as amusing and entertaining as possible.

I have gone into the welcome you get at this particular house in detail because it's the welcome you give your guests which starts off the whole week end. Can there be anything more dreary than to arrive to stay several days at a house where there is only a bored-looking servant to receive you (and not one who has been taught to *smile*)? Or to drive up to a tightly shut door and have to ring the doorbell or pound the knocker to let your hosts know that you are standing forlornly on their doorstep? At such times (and probably they have happened to you; I know they have happened to *me*) you feel readier to turn tail and run away than to stick it out until Sunday evening.

After all, to ask people to your house to spend the week end is a much greater compliment than just asking them to luncheon or to dinner or to drop in some afternoon for a game of bridge. It implies that you are friends. Or at least there is a good prospect of your becoming so. Since you have asked them in advance and know just when they are arriving, there's no excuse possible for your not being there to welcome them when they *do* come.

Also, if they come late in the afternoon and dinner is not ready until much later you will want to have tea and other drinks ready to offer them the minute they arrive and after they have been upstairs to see their rooms. If there are children in the family they will enjoy welcoming the guests with you and passing the plates of thin bread and butter or whatever you have with the tea.

In playing this fascinating game of week-ending the first move is up to you as hostess. This is the letter which you send to ask your friends to come. The real appeal of such an invitation is its spontaneity, of course. But there are seven pointers which such a letter should contain. All of

them are vitally necessary to the success of the week end for you and your guests. See if you can find them in the following letter which I offer as a suggestion, not as a model:

LITTLE BROOK FARM

July 17, 1940

DEAR SARAH,

Won't you and Bob come out to the farm on Friday afternoon, arriving about six o'clock, and stay until Sunday evening?

We'll have a quiet evening just by ourselves on Friday; on Saturday there's a tennis tournament, and that evening a few people are coming in to dine informally here before we all go on to a dance at the club.

For the rest of the week end we'll swim and relax rurally.

I suppose you'll drive out. But, if not, there's a good train to Ridgefield (our station) from the Grand Central at 4:37.

Do come. Harry and I are longing to see you both.

Affectionately yours,<br>EDITH MERRINGTON

P.S.   Our telephone number is Ridgefield oo.

If you will go over this very carefully you're sure to discover the seven vital points. These are:

1. It tells just *when* you expect your guest.
2. It says *for how long* you invite her to stay.
3. It tells *how to get there* by train as well as by motor.
4. It *lists the proposed activities* so that she and Bob will bring the right clothes.
5. It tells that the week end will not be so filled with activities that the guests will be tired out rather than refreshed by it.
6. It is written so cordially that there is no mistaking the welcome that awaits them from their hostess and host.

7. It gives the telephone number so in case they cannot accept the invitation they can let the hostess know this *immediately*, thus allowing her to ask another couple in their place.

For many reasons a hostess wants to keep her week-end party balanced, with an equal number of men and women. Knowing this, Sarah does not reply that she will come with pleasure but "don't expect Bob as he is going on a fishing trip with some men."

A week-end party is like a salad: perfect when it combines the right ingredients in the right measure, but devastating if any of the wrong ingredients get in. Think what one tired radish can do to an otherwise palate-tantalizing bowlful of greens! Just one person who is too argumentative or who doesn't fit in with the others can turn a houseful of guests upside down. Because of this you will want to make your week-end combinations as carefully as you mix your salads. You may want most awfully to ask Jane (who has just been divorced), but unless you have an extra, unattached man coming for the same week end *don't*. However fond you may be of Jane, don't ask her to bring a man with her. In the first place, *no man ever wants to be taken anywhere by a woman*, no matter how devoted to her he may be. (You won't be helping Jane's cause with this particular man to suggest it.) Also, you have to think of your party as a whole. Jane's beau may seem terribly attractive to her. But at the same time he may be just a tired radish to the other ingredients of your bowl.

And of course, no matter how informal the week end is to be, no woman would think of going to stay in any house unless she has been specially invited by the hostess herself.

Why wait till Thursday to ask your friends to spend the week end with you? Your women friends will want to plan their clothes for the visit and for the entertainment you have in store for them. It's quite possible they may want the fun of getting some brand-new things just for the occasion. Who wants to have to stop the taxi on the way to the train in order to snatch a bathing suit—and in that rush—*any* bathing suit—from a shop counter? Women want to be able to pack their things carefully. They want to be sure that they have everything they are going to need for the week end.

And you don't want to have to hunt out beach coats, woolen stockings, sweaters and sneakers for guests who have been too rushed or too careless to bring their own along with them.

## Getting the House Ready for the Week End

RIGHT HERE is where all those important details we talked about which make your house say welcome come in.

Starting at the front door, go through your hall, living room and up-stairs to the guest's room and bath, looking at everything with an eagle eye.

Is there a really inviting air about your front door?

Is your living room really *livable?* Will everyone who comes into it feel comfortable and at home right away? You have asked these friends to spend several days with you. No one finds it much fun to spend a week end in a house which may be furnished with museum pieces of antique furniture but which hasn't a single deep, comfortable chair or a big long sofa on which to drop down with a magazine or a book. Personally I'd be as happy spending the week end in the American Wing at the Metropolitan Art Museum.

Have you some new and interesting and unusual magazines lying about for guests to amuse themselves with in between whiles? Have you ordered the extra newspaper for your guest's breakfast tray?

Have you plenty of cigarettes of several brands? Matches? Many convenient ash trays?

What about the supply of liquor? Also ginger ale, Coca-Cola, lemons and fruit juices?

And under the trees are there some *comfortable chairs*, freshly painted (but not so recently that the paint comes off on an unsuspecting guest)? Are there plenty of cushions and several of those roll-up narrow mattresses on which to lie on the grass or on the beach in the sun, or under the stars? (You can get these at any of the department stores for two dollars and less.)

Upstairs, has the guest's room all the things to make her stay luxuriously comfortable? I've already pictured a perfect guest room. If you want to add to this how about a small radio? And an electric, plug-in telephone connection? (How your guest will bless you.) It goes without saying that a guest always pays for her own long-distance telephone calls. A screen is a great convenience in a guest room for those who like to sleep late and who are disturbed by sunlight. They can arrange the screen between the windows and the bed.

Quite a number of very happily married couples do not sleep comfortably in the same room. (Alas! the husband may snore.) If you are not asking any other guests you may be able to give the husband and wife separate rooms. If not why not do as a very clever bachelor I know does —have four or five tents set up on wooden platforms behind the house? When he asks a number of people out to his place in Connecticut for the week end the women stay in the house with his mother. Bachelors and any husbands who like the idea sleep in the tents. There's a bathroom on the lower floor of the house with a door opening into it from the outside for the tent dwellers.

## Getting Yourself Ready

THIS IS EVERY BIT as important as getting your house in order for weekend entertaining. This is what makes week-end entertaining fun for the hostess.

Immediately after you've decided to ask some friends down to spend that week end with you, and have written or rung them up to invite them, it's time to start planning your fun, so as not to have to fuss later on. Have you exactly the right clothes to wear for all the activities you have planned? If you haven't, then set about getting them right away. If it's to be a week end in slacks and sweater then why not get yourself a brand-new and outrageously gay bandana to wear around your neck or to tie up your hair? Make your week-end party an excuse to get yourself some new, bright-colored espadrilles. And because it's *your* party is no reason why you should come out in a faded, unbecoming bathing suit.

See that all the clothes you will need for the week end are in perfect order and ready for you to hop into them at a moment's notice. Sew the fresh frills on your dress; don't wait to have to do this while the car is at the door and everyone is calling you to hurry up.

Carry your preparedness program into the kitchen. Plan all the meals for the entire week end, and do the marketing on Friday if your guests are coming that afternoon. Don't let it run over to be done in the busy hours of Saturday morning. Get plenty of the food you intend to have.

Remember our rule (I've stressed it again and again), smart entertaining is simple, *but it is done with a flair*. No fussy foods. No elaborate menus which put a strain on the cook's temper and the guests' patience. Plain food, but perfect of its kind. And plenty of it, even though only two courses. Week-end guests who go in for exercise on the golf links or in the water develop healthy appetites.

In that same household which I pictured for you a little while back, in which the husband does all the cooking, dinner (or rather supper) never consists of more than three courses. And no meat, for economy's sake. There is a very rich and filling soup, which the host serves himself from a big tureen into bowls and of which there is enough for two helpings all around. This may be clam chowder, corn chowder, lobster bisque, borsch or a French all-vegetable soup with freshly grated Parmesan cheese. After this comes a big wooden bowl of green and vegetable with, perhaps, a cheese soufflé. Then fruit and coffee. All very simple to prepare and to serve. But *lots* of everything. They always have a long, crisp French loaf and *plenty* of delicious fresh butter, pressed into little pats with a design on them. (You can buy the wood shapes and do up a whole pound of butter at a time.)

In most localities there are special local dishes which make use of foods grown or caught near by. These foods are usually cheaper than the things which are shipped in from distant markets. And your guests who come out from the city will enjoy eating them on their native heath.

So if you live by the seashore, go in for clam pie and clam chowder. Learn a number of lobster dishes that you can spring on your friends when they come for a week end. Practice until you can make absolutely perfect codfish cakes.

If your home is along the Eastern Shore you don't need to be reminded how good deviled crabs can be.

Inland there are memorable American dishes to be made out of vegetables and some of the inexpensive cuts of meat. In Bucks County, Penn., there's a famous pie, made of home-grown raspberries and sour cream that is treat enough for one week end.

## Week-End Amusements

OF COURSE you will have thought of this part of the week-end fun even before you asked your friends to come.

Today most of us are exercise-minded. We all want to enter into sports and to play games. Especially those of us who are in business and who work hard all through the week look forward to the hours between Friday afternoon and Sunday night as a time when we can stretch our muscles and play our favorite sports.

If you ask friends to spend the week end with you it is to be presumed that you are prepared to give them plenty of opportunities for exercise (if they want this). You may be lucky enough to have your own water front for bathing and boating or even your own pool for swimming. If you have the space for them why not start saving up for your own tennis or badminton courts? Playing these games at home is so much more fun than on club courts.

Of course you may belong to a country club which offers all these delights. In this case it is easy for you to take your week-end guests over to the club for sports.

If there is a good club near you, and you don't belong to it (you may be economizing this summer), then perhaps you have a friend who *does* belong and who will put your guests up at the club for the week end. Arrange for this before your guests arrive. And whether you belong to the club or your guests are put up there by your friend, *the guests pay their own green fees and their own caddies.*

It may be that one or two of the friends you have asked down for the week end are terribly keen about golf and play well. In this case find out if there happens to be a tombstone tournament at the club that week in which they can enter. If so put their names down in time. Or if tennis, arrange this also.

But don't, on any account, cram the week end too full. Most people want some time in which to be alone, to lie on a comfortable sofa with a book, to go for a walk by themselves, to talk with their hosts. Leave some room for the entertainment to shape itself—everyone will get more fun out of the week end if you do.

Above all, give your guests the greatest hospitality of all, the feeling that they may do as *they like. Even doing nothing.*

If you're planning a winter week end be sure to let your guests know whether there will be any skiing so they can bring their skis and skiing clothes. And why not take advantage of winter week ends when the snow is just right to open up your country house or camp and ask a houseful of friends out for winter sports?

Even if you don't own a country place yet you could rent some land in hilly country and put up a cabin there that would make an ideal spot for skiing week ends. The furnishings should be as crude as you like—only be sure to have lots of fur rugs for the floor (you can get them for under five dollars at most department stores), comfortable chairs to draw around the fire (you could have these covered with corduroy, tweed or cowhide) and plenty of light, warm, bright-colored blankets for the bunks where you and your friends will sleep. I describe a week-end one-room bunkhouse like this in my book *Decorating Is Fun*.

## What If It Rains?

SINCE ALL SPORTS are more or less dependent on fine weather it's the better part of wisdom, when planning a week end, to take into account that it may rain. In this case you and your guests will have to amuse your-selves indoors.

Keep a supply of games—checkers, backgammon, chess, cribbage, dom-inoes, parchesi—to be brought out for such emergencies. And a shelf of not-too-old detective stories. Learn or invent some games which can be played with paper and pencils. Any quick-witted group of friends will promptly develop their own form of Consequences, Twenty Questions or one of the popular psychological quizzes.

If your house has an attic why not keep an old trunk there filled with old clothes to be brought out for charades during a rainy week end?

And you can have a lot of fun sitting around the dining table playing the old favorite, Up Jenkins. If your dining table is a prized antique it is better to play this on the ping-pong table in the game room. Or even in the kitchen, where bangs and thumps will do no damage.

Then you can wind up the evening with an old-fashioned candy pull.

## Rooms for Fun

NOWADAYS, with cellars and attics blossoming out into game rooms, what was once the coalbin may now house a billiard or ping-pong table, a bar and a workable putting green.

The ideal game room, whether you find room for it at the top of the house, in the basement or in the loft over the garage, is planned to stand hard wear and tear. If you cover the floor with black or dark green linoleum you can stencil a shuffleboard on it and then wax it. After that you can dance on it, do yoga exercises, play all sorts of games and never worry a wrinkle if anyone spills hot coffee or beer.

Ideally, too, a game room should have an open fireplace. If it hasn't see if you can't make up for this lack by installing a generous-sized stove.

If you and your family are dramatically inclined then build a small but workable stage across one end of the game room and go in for amateur theatricals. Or at least charades. If any member of the family is a movie-camera fan arrange for a screen so he can show his pictures. And of course the room needs a good radio and a victrola for dancing.

A table for ping-pong, several card tables (these can be folded away in a cupboard when not in use). Several big, comfortable sofas or cushioned seats against the walls and a dozen or so light, fold-up chairs and tables (also to be kept in the cupboard) are necessities. So are at least four good, plain lamps with high-powered bulbs.

## Luxury on Little

SPEAKING FOR MYSELF, I don't enjoy being asked to be a week-end guest and to be put to work by my hostess. Please don't ask me to paint the furniture or spray the roses or carry stones for a rock garden. If you insist on asking me to do these things I'll probably do them. But I won't enjoy them or my visit.

But after all, that's just my personal feelings. You may feel quite differently about it. And your friends may think it's lots of fun to chop wood, help build the swimming pool and a new chimney or anything else that is really hard work.

Not long ago I heard of a young couple who bought a very much run-down farm in Connecticut. They hadn't much money to rebuild the house and other buildings or to clear and plant the grounds. But they had lots of friends as young as themselves and as enthusiastic. The farm owners spent twenty-five dollars or so laying in a stock of blue jeans and colored shirts of all sizes, sneakers of assorted sizes and big straw hats and bandanas. These they hung in the barn. The guests were asked to bring only a tiny bag with their night things, no clothes. When the friends arrived for the week end they were led immediately to the barn and fitted out in farm clothes. After that they were ready for work. The guests enjoyed it and everyone had the feeling of a fancy-dress week end.

Not everyone is as eager to be turned into a handy man or woman. A lot of your friends may be like me. They, too, may want to be as comfortable during the week end as they are in their own homes during the rest of the time. (I like camping out, but that is different.)

My own conviction is that this leads us right back to that all-important question: *what do you think is worth spending money for?* What will give everyone the most fun for the money? You may feel that having one or two friends visit you over the week end necessitates spending money for large and expensive meals, for wines and cigars, expensive, imported cheeses and other table luxuries. I don't. I would rather economize on these things and have two dollars to hire a part-time maid at fifty cents an hour to come in on the afternoon when the guests arrive to unpack them and to press the clothes that need pressing and again on the day they leave to repack their bags. (The guests will bless you.) If this isn't possible in your community it's a simple thing to put a small folding ironing board and an electric iron in the guest's bathroom. You could put up a notice something like this:

> SORRY. NO EXPERT LADY'S MAID IN ATTENDANCE
> IRONING BOARD AND IRON WILL BE FOUND IN BATHROOM

## You Can't Get 'Em Up!

ANOTHER LUXURY which most week-end guests appreciate is not to be expected to get up for breakfast. Surely there's no tremendous effort involved in carrying a pretty breakfast tray with fruit, coffee and buttered toast or a hot roll upstairs to the guest's room. If you have no maid to do this do it yourself. Or train one of the children to do it. Most children love to do things that are really of use and which give them a satisfying sense of responsibility.

The breakfast tray should be as fresh and dainty as a flower. What guest does not appreciate gay flowered or polka-dotted china? This does not have to be expensive. Investigate the counters in the ten-cent store. But everything on the tray should match. The tray cloth should be absolutely crisp and immaculate. Tray cloths of organdy, either white, with appliqué designs in a pale color to match the breakfast china, or flowered organdy with wide, plain borders are charming. Or simple

white with lace edge. These are easy to make, too, so you can have a
number of them.

Men guests, who mutter menacingly at mention of breakfast in bed,
can be told the night before that there will be a buffet breakfast in the
dining room from nine o'clock on. Leave them to serve themselves to hot
or cold cereal, bacon, coffee, fruit and toast whenever they choose.
Here is another use for your electric grill, Toastmaster and hot-water
dishes.

By having a buffet breakfast when you have week-end guests your
maid (if you have one) is not interrupted in her regular morning schedule. You, your husband and the children can have your own family
breakfast by yourselves (there's no reason why guests staying in the
house should put an end to family life), and your guests will enjoy being
able to sleep as long as they feel like doing.

If you have a small house and no maid to consider and like to have
week-end guests you can arrange a buffet for breakfast in the upper hall.
A big thermos bottle of chilled orange juice, another of hot coffee, a
small thermos jug of cream, sugar, cups and saucers, glasses, an electric
toaster and a covered plate of slices of bread set out on a table in the
upstairs hall for guests to help themselves whenever they wake up and
want breakfast isn't any trouble at all. You can use your wheeled tea
table for this purpose most satisfactorily. Get some tin trays at the ten-
cent store, paint them pretty colors and let each person carry her breakfast back to her bed.

Of course there's always the bedmaking problem when guests linger
late abed. If this habit puts too heavy a strain on your domestic economy
why not take the bedmaking duties on your own hands over the week

end. Or put it up to your guests themselves. After all, it's a poor sort of guest who won't gladly make her own bed for the privilege of remaining in it as long as she likes.

## Dutch-Treat Week Ends

SUPPOSE YOU HAVE a small house and a small income and lots of friends and an enormous bump of hospitality. The problem then presents itself how to juggle these into some fun for yourself and your friends over week ends.

If there's even a fairly good inn near by you could tell your friends frankly that if they would like to come down and put themselves up there for the week end you would adore having them take their meals with you and join you in playing games and sports.

Or, lacking the inn, you could reserve several cabins at a near-by tourist camp for your week-end guests. They would pay for the cabins themselves. And gladly, if they know that week-ending with you and your husband is *fun*.

Have you ever thought of getting two or three husbands and wives to take their cars and all of you going off for a Dutch-treat week end, exploring some part of the country you have never seen before? You could discover Cape Cod or little-known bits of Long Island. You could explore the Shenandoah Valley or learn your country's history firsthand in and about Williamsburg, Virginia.

Trips like these don't cost much if you stay at tourist homes or camps and patronize the small places for meals.

And they can be a lot of fun when six or eight good friends take them together. One of you can be responsible for looking up the route. Another makes the overnight arrangements and is treasurer, telephoning or wiring ahead for reservations. Someone else is expected to be up on the history and interesting information about the country you go to see. And another sees that there are cards, Chinese checkers, a backgammon board and dominoes to play games when you are all together in the evenings.

## How to Be a Good Week-Ender

So FAR everything we have said has been pointed to the hostess. But this chapter applies to the week-end guest as well.

First, you have the pleasure of being in a different and lovely house long enough to get the real feel of it and of the life which is lived within its walls. That in itself is a great privilege and always rather exciting, I think.

In those forty-eight hours or so between Friday evening and when you leave late on Sunday there's time to be alone and to relax in an environment where there is nothing of your own everyday life crying out to you for attention. There's the opportunity for an all-alone-by-your-selves visit with your hostess who may be an old friend whom you're terribly fond of and don't have a chance to see as often as you would wish. Or she may be a new and interesting acquaintance whom you hope to know better. The week end is a time for cementing old friendships and for making new ones. People who spend two whole days together, who play and laugh and talk together, get to know each other very well indeed.

Even marriages, which used to be made in heaven, are now conceded to be made over week ends.

If you are a week-end guest certain definite things are expected of you.

1. You will arrive promptly at the time indicated in your hostess's invitation. (And don't change the hour.)

2. You will bring with you everything you expect to wear and need during the visit. There's nothing so troublemaking as a borrower.

3. You will not bring so much luggage and such heavy bags that your host (if you happen to know there are no manservants) is hard put to it to carry them up to your room.

4. You will accept and enthusiastically agree in the plans your hostess has made for your and her entertainment.

5. You will not be a "yes, yes" guest. That is, you will say truthfully and at once whether you would rather play golf or tennis, swim now or go for a walk and swim later.

6. You will pull your own weight over the week end. That is, you will have taken pains well in advance to brush up your tennis and your bridge game so that your hosts and their other friends will find you fun to be with. Save up one or two new and amusing stories to contribute to the talk around the dinner table on the night you arrive.

7. If you come by train and your hosts have no car in which to meet you take a taxi at the station *and pay for this yourself*. If you come in your own car and there is no room for it in your hosts' garage they will arrange for the car to be taken care of in the public garage near by. *But you will pay the expense of this yourself.*

8. Of course you will pay for all long-distance telephone calls and charges on telegrams. If you are taken to the club to play golf you pay your own caddy and also your green fees.

9. When you leave you will tip the servants who have waited on you (giving the largest tip to the maid who has pressed your clothes, brought your breakfast and unpacked and packed your bag). In a large household it is not usual for guests to tip the cook. But if there is only

one maid of all work you will go out to the kitchen to thank her for her part in making your stay so pleasant and tip her. It may be that she would prefer to have you send her a little present, like a bag, after you return home.

10. When you reach home, and as immediately as possible, you will write your hostess to thank her for the fun you have had over the week end. You may, if you wish (and personally I think it's a nice gesture), send her some small and not expensive gift. This might be a book she has expressed a longing to read. A new game you think she and her family will enjoy. Some plants or rare seeds for her garden. Or a new really labor-saving household gadget you think she hasn't seen yet.


## CASE HISTORY OF A LADY WHO FOUND OUT THERE ARE FIFTY–TWO WEEK ENDS IN EVERY YEAR

Every year between Thanksgiving and Christmas Mrs R—— was in the habit of closing her country house, leaving a caretaker and his wife in the kitchen wing, and coming to town until the blossoming of the dogwood and lilacs gave her the signal that she could go back to the country again.

Every year she looked forward to the time when she would have to close the country house with a heavy heart. And every year, even in her lovely little Sutton Place house with its river view, she counted the days on her desk calendar until she could go back to the country.

It wasn't just the country she longed for. Or being in her own house that she had lived in for years and years. It was having a place to ask her friends to, especially over week ends. True, she could see those friends in town. But in the city people were always so rushed. When they came together they seemed to find it impossible to relax. They made conversation determinedly instead of just letting conversation *happen*.

That was what Mrs R—— liked especially about week-end parties. Something invariably happened at them. From Friday to Sunday night relationships developed, grew, changed. The people who went away after a week end were just a little different from what they were like when they came.

"Dear me," she said to herself one day when she was looking forward to a rather prosaic Friday to Monday in the city, "I wish week ends could go on all through the year."

And immediately she got her big idea.

Last summer she had taken a cure at Baden-Baden and had come away feeling full of zest for living. Why, she had wondered then, shouldn't week ends in the country send people back to town feeling like that? Now she said to herself, "They can." There was her big roomy house (it had a furnace which heated it adequately plus roaring fires in the open fireplaces) and a caretaker's wife who was noted for being "willing." There were snow fields for skiing and the lake for skating. There could be long walks and everyone could be privileged to go to bed as early as ten o'clock if they wished.

Mrs R—— wrote and telephoned to six friends of hers, asking them to her house in the country for a "catch-as-catch-can" week end, two weeks off.

"What in the world does 'catch-as-catch-can' mean?" they demanded.

"I'm sending you directions," was all she would tell them. The next day each guest received by mail a copy of the following "directions."

When her guests arrived the first thing they saw in the familiar front hall was a large blackboard. On this were written their names and after each name a chore, as:

TONY.........................Keep all wood boxes filled.
                            Woodpile behind the kitchen door.

PETER.........................See that all ash trays are emptied.
                            Also see skates, skis, sleds are
                            put away in good order.

BOB............................Tend bar.

MARY.........................Set table.

ANNE and JANE..................Make beds.

MRS. R—— .....................Keep living room in order.

In several places about the house the guests discovered small type-written notices, such as:

BATHROOM MANNERS
Don't use all the hot water, if there
happens to be any
(Remember, others are as dirty as you.)
Note the color of your bath towels
and
P-LE-ASE Pick Up the Soap!

The first "catch-as-catch-can" week end was a terrific success. Everyone ate huge quantities of the delicious plain food—corn chowder, baked beans, roast beef, baked potatoes, cole slaw, gingerbread, apple pie—

which the willing caretaker's wife cooked. Everyone enjoyed doing the chores and took pride in doing them perfectly.

No one asked for substitutions or for breakfasts in bed. No one, that is, except Anne. (Mrs R—— was quite right about relationships growing and changing over week ends.) Anne flatly refused to get up for breakfast. She said to Tony, who had been terribly devoted to her for years, "You can bring my tray up to me at ten o'clock."

Promptly at ten Tony rapped on Anne's door. He came in, carrying a perfect poem of a breakfast tray, all rosy-flowered china on a pale pink linen cloth. There was the covered coffeepot, a covered milk jug, a cup and saucer and a covered dish for the hot toast. He greeted her gaily (let us hope he gave her a kiss), set the tray on her knees and departed. Anne smiled happily. She lifted the coffeepot, then the cover of the toast dish. There was absolutely nothing to eat or drink!

Mrs R—— was quite right about relationships growing and changing over week ends. Tony is now married to Mary (who came down to breakfast). They are frequent guests at Mrs R——'s "catch-as-catch-can" week-end parties, for she has gone on having them during the winter months and sometimes in summer too. Her friends just won't let her give them up.

# 9

## ENTERTAINING OUT OF DOORS

### Romance Preferred

Whenever i have been away from my penthouse apartment in New York, if it is in summer, the first thing I do is to go to the big window in the living room and look down. There, in that one block, are at least nine roof terraces, balconies and back-yard gardens. There, during the warm weather months, the owners dine, breakfast, play games, take sun baths, do setting-up exercises, garden and entertain their friends. They present a number of different ideas for making the outdoors livable. Anyone with a tiny garden plot behind the house or even a stretch of roof to turn into a terrace could do something along these lines.

In the past few years city dwellers have gone a little mad on the subject of roofs, terraces and penthouses. There's a general movement to do as much of our living as possible in the open.

A friend and I have given the owners of those outdoor living rooms names and histories. First there is the lady we call the "Romantic Lady."

## The Romantic Lady's Garden

THIS WAS ONCE just a back yard where housemaids hung out the laundry. Then the house was turned into apartments and the Romantic Lady rented the lowest floor. She laid a terrace of roofing tiles just outside the back door, set out some white-painted tables and chairs and shaded it with a white-painted lattice which, in summer, is veiled with blue-flowered Mexican morning glories.

The high fence around the back yard is also painted white, and along it grows a shrubbery of lilac, syringa, forsythia and rose of Sharon, with a ribbon of spring-flowering bulbs at their feet.

In the center of the yard is a grass plot with a broad tree of heaven under which the Romantic Lady sets her tea table on Monday afternoons when she is "at home." She wears long, trailing, pale-colored frocks and big, floppy, flower-wreathed hats and looks quite worthy the name we have given her.

Her Mondays evidently are quite popular, and her friends seem to enjoy the garden and her enthusiastically.

## The General's Balcony

IT'S JUST a small balcony, but it has a pleasing Victorian curve and a really lovely wrought-iron railing around it. A long double window opens onto it. Over it the general has put up a semicircular awning of broad red-and-white stripes with a scalloped edge (it's rather like one half of a huge umbrella). Brackets fixed to the brick house wall hold pots of trailing ivy. Other pots of ivy are fastened to the balcony railing and the green vines run along it delightfully. A pair of tall standard fuchsias in green-and-white painted tubs, two Chinese wicker chairs and a small low wicker table complete the furniture.

There the general has his breakfast each morning. There he sits to read the Sunday newspaper and there he entertains his grandchildren on their weekly visits. Frequently when the summer afternoon is tapering into evening he and a friend sit comfortably and sip their mint juleps. (At least I am sure the drinks *must* be juleps.)

## The Sun-Deckers

THE COUPLE with the sun deck are evidently of a nautical turn of mind. They have covered the roof outside their apartment with tarpaulin and railed it in with white painted rope laced through white painted wooden posts. They have hung a pair of life preservers on either side of the door and above these two shining brass ship's lanterns fitted with electric lights. Blue canvas deck chairs and a white canvas hammock with blue cushions complete the picture. They give parties there all summer long. They play shuffleboard and quoits and deck tennis exactly as if they and their guests were cruising somewhere in tropical seas. They wheel out a white painted serving wagon which is fitted with blue-and-white steins for beer, a covered tray for cheese and a covered board for a loaf of dark pumpernickel.

## Memories of Mexico

IT MUST HAVE BEEN a patio somewhere south of the Rio Grande that provided the inspiration for the roof garden whose owner we call Mrs Greatheart. This roof garden is sheltered by a high fence of woven cypress wood. On metal supports across the roof, well above the top of the fence, are laid bamboo screens, arranged so that they can be drawn back close to the house wall after dark when the moon is coming up. In the corners of the garden are orange trees in tubs. Plants of lantana and calendulas grow in pots fastened to the fence. In the center is a circular flower bed (a carpenter made the wooden frame a foot deep which is filled with rich earth) and this is a glowing mass of yellow-and-orange-flowered tuberous begonias. There is a big, luxurious double chaise longue with bright lemon-yellow cushions, on wheels, which can be pushed about, allowing Mrs Greatheart to lie with her back to the sun. And two other canvas-covered chairs. There is a strong wooden drop-leaf table painted Spanish blue. A great many young people, young men and girls, come to see Mrs Greatheart, who is evidently a sympathetic sort. They have long talks in the patio. Frequently Mrs Greatheart has one or two of them to lunch with her there. She brings out the tablecloth, glasses, china, silver and the food on a blue painted tray which fits on a support (rather like a trunk rest) and acts as a serving table.

## A Triangle for Two

FOR A LONG TIME the apartment with the triangular bit of roof outside it was vacant. Then, late in the autumn, curtains and lights appeared at the windows. On the first warm day in April the windows were flung up and a young woman clambered out onto the roof. She stood and looked around her the way Balboa may have looked at the Pacific. Not even Balboa could have had more imagination or verve. When next seen the young woman was up on a stepladder, painting the outside wall of the house between her windows white. A few days later she had a carpenter out there making a deep flower box fourteen inches wide and fastening this along the slanting edge of her triangle of roof. This, too, she painted white. The box was filled with earth and a hedge of privet was planted in it. Against the white painted house wall she set big red clay flowerpots with vigorous plants of euonymous. When the weather seemed settled the young woman brought out an old kitchen table (perhaps from the thrift shop around the corner). The legs and underpinning of this she painted a lovely sky blue. The top she covered with oilcloth. Next came two white canvas chairs, a solid wooden kitchen chair, also painted sky blue, and a really huge blue-and-white-striped garden umbrella which covered nearly the whole roof. Finally the young woman hung a big round Della Robia plaque (white figures on a blue ground and framed in a wreath of white sculptured fruits) on the white brick wall.

My friend and I were not surprised to see two of the chairs under the big umbrella occupied on most evenings and on Sundays. A very tall young man seemed to get a great deal of enjoyment clipping the privet hedge and training the euonymous to grow around the Della Robia plaque. The young woman seemed to enjoy bringing out two blue trays set with white china from which she and the young man dined, cafeteria fashion. Sometimes they played Russian bank on the blue-and-silver table which was lighted by a pair of tall hurricane lamps.

My friend and I have no doubt but that it will be a very happy marriage.

## Protection from Glare—and Neighbors

ON ALL CITY ROOF GARDENS awnings are practically a necessity, not only to cut down the hot glare but also to protect the cushions and chairs from the fall of soot which goes on constantly. Therefore the problem immediately arises: how to keep awnings clean. The roof garden should have a water connection and a faucet to which a garden hose can be attached, and then the garden and awnings can be hosed down every day. This does much to cool the rooms inside, and if you have plants in the garden you will have the delicious, cool smell of the wet foliage. Plant some plants just for fragrance—heliotrope (which does well in pots), lemon verbena, nicotiana with its sweet-scented white trumpet flowers. And that most fragrant of all the stocks—*mathiola bicornis*. It's nothing at all to look at—rather spindly and pale and ineffectual. But after dark it sends forth a perfume which inspires romance in the most unpromising quarters.

Be color-shrewd when you select your awnings. Remember orange is *hot*. Red, on the other hand—especially red piped or lined with white —is gay and refreshing. Broad stripes of green and white or blue and white or lemon yellow and white are charming. Or you can have plain white (and hose them every day). Or any plain color that appeals to you.

You can shade your terrace with white painted Venetian blinds which let in the air and interesting slanting rays of light.

## If You Live Out of Town

Everyone who has a real garden knows the advantage of having some part of it arranged to use at times as an outdoor living room. This may be a bench and a table under an apple tree where you and your husband can breakfast deliciously on Sunday mornings, where you give the children occasional cambric-tea parties and where you can take the friend who drops in to see you in the hot part of the afternoon.

It may be an angle of garden, walled by shrubbery so it is completely private, where you can set out a white painted table and serve a buffet Sunday-night supper. Your guests will be comfortable in white painted wooden chairs, the kind with deep, backward-slanting seats and very broad arms, wide enough to hold a plate and a glass.

A wheeled serving wagon will bring the food out from the kitchen and make a party out of doors no more trouble than one right in the house. An amusing gay note is furnished if the wagon is one of the parti-colored hurdy-gurdy carts which make you think of the first act of *Pagliacci*. Or you can be thrifty and original at the same time and buy a good-sized child's express wagon and paint this yourself in any combination of colors that seem to you festive.

Food served out of doors calls for quite different containers and china than you would use for parties indoors. Hunt the ten-cent stores for wooden bowls, trays, serving spoons, etc. You can get Mexican pottery very inexpensively. This is most effective on an outdoor buffet. When you go shopping for fittings for the picnic basket remember the advantages of unbreakable plates and cups.

## A Playhouse

OUR VICTORIAN ANCESTORS *adored* summerhouses. The ones I remember were earwiggy affairs, vine-hung and rather gloomy. The ladies sat in them with their fancy work or reading, and it was generally believed that proposals happened there.

Today instead of the summerhouse we have the garden playhouse. This may be open on all four sides, as the summerhouse was, but furnished with comfortable chairs, tables for games and for meals out of doors. It may have an open fireplace where you can broil a steak or toast frankfurters. A cupboard can hold a small but practical electric stove and on the shelves above this plates and cups and saucers of some strong, colorful peasant pottery, knives and forks with colored composition handles, glasses and serving dishes.

The reason why entertaining out of doors seems to some women more of an effort than entertaining in the house is because they think it necessitates a lot of carrying of things back and forth. The clever thing to do is to fit yourself out with a complete service for outdoor parties (from the ten-cent store or elsewhere) and to keep this in some convenient place. And *only* for these occasions.


## A Playhouse on the Dunes

WHEN MY FRIENDS' seaside house was burned down everyone who knew them fully expected that they would promptly rebuild it. But they did nothing of the sort. Instead they fitted up an apartment over the garage (which had escaped the fire) in which they are quite comfortable. And on the peak of the dunes, literally at the edge of the sea, they built a one-room playhouse. This has the side toward the ocean all of glass with a cushioned bench just inside it where you can lie and watch the sun set. It has an open fireplace for driftwood fires on damp days. In the recesses on each side of the fireplace are built-in bunks (useful for week-end guests). Shutter doors conceal these from view when not in use. At the opposite end of the room is an electrically equipped kitchenette. Just outside, and connected with the house by a short, covered passageway, are two bathhouses with fresh-water showers.

The playhouse on the dunes is the perfect place for beach parties. In one of its cupboards are canvas-covered, roll-up mattresses which can be thrown down on the sand, beach umbrellas, bathing suits, towels and several big red rubber balls for games on the sand and in the water.

My friends give parties there all the time and everyone has a *grand* time.

Even if you live elsewhere it might be possible to lease a spot on the dunes and have such a playhouse as this for week ends and holidays.

## For California Nights

As NEARLY EVERYONE KNOWS, the Napa Valley, north of San Francisco, has long been celebrated for its wines. A young couple who live in Berkeley scouted up and down the valley until they found an abandoned winery. This was a big square stone building, from which the roof was long since gone. It was built against the side of a hill, and an arched doorway led into a deep cave where the wine casks used to lie. The vineyards which had supplied the winery had been sold. There was left only a small plot of land and the abandoned building.

The young couple bought this. They cleared the rubbish out of the shell and found, underneath this, a concrete floor. They patched some of the holes in the walls (leaving others for picturesque effect). Against one wall, inside the shell, they built a one-story lean-to which they divided into bedroom, bath and tiny kitchen. The walls were made of wire screening with Venetian blinds on the inside. They had a carpenter make solid wooden shutters to clamp on on the outside when they are away. And during the rainy season.

In one corner of the big open-roofed winery they built a huge fireplace, with a grill for broiling and a spit and a crane from which they hung an iron kettle. They built two long benches of redwood and made for these long cushions upholstered in Irish-green tweed. They made trestles of redwood and fastened these to the concrete floor. The redwood table top is laid on these. Several deep open shelves fastened to the concrete wall and protected with a little slanting roof hold red and yellow pottery bowls, plates and serving dishes.

They have supper there every Sunday evening and any number of their friends may drop in on them. Supper is always simple and made up of dishes which can be added to as more guests arrive. One of the favorites is Mediterranean stew. This is made of big pieces of eggplant and tomatoes, peppers and onions cut into quarters, all simmered in the iron pot over the fire in a cupful of olive oil and seasoned with thyme, basil and part of a clove of garlic.

## A Small House and a Big Swimming Pool

THAT, one couple decided, constituted the perfect home. So they built one. The house was tiny: just two small bedrooms, bath, a living room that was more cozy than generous and a kitchen. It was made of brick, painted white, with a flat roof, high ceilings and a charming porch of Charleston grilles. (And all on an F.H.A. loan.) A broad flagstone walk led from the house to the swimming pool, which was big enough for a dozen swimmers to practice strokes in at a time. The flagstone walk ran around the pool and at the far end is a little three-sided shelter. The open side toward the pool was fitted with garage doors that swing up and fit inside the roof.

I don't know anything gayer than that swimming pool all summer long. There are big comfortable wooden chairs (the seats are made of slats so you can drip through). There are a number of canvas-covered roll-up mattresses to lie on and sun yourself after a swim. There are big bright-colored garden umbrellas. Inside the shelter is a good radio and an electric icebox in which the beer is kept.

A red-and-yellow hurdy-gurdy cart does duty as a bar.

People begin to arrive about eleven o'clock on Sunday morning and the party by the pool goes on until midnight. Then the mattresses, cushions, umbrellas, etc., are put away in the shelter; the doors are locked, and host and hostess go back to their small house which has been undisturbed by the party.

## A Cabana by the Sea

THERE'S SOMETHING irresistibly romantic about a cabana, even when it's just a second-hand army tent, painted bright blue with the addition of big red-and-white tassels and set up on a bluff looking out to sea. The owners rent the privilege of camping there for fifty dollars a season. Every Friday evening they drive out to it from their jobs in town. Air mattresses make comfortable beds. A waterproof chest holds bedding and camping-out clothes. A rain barrel set outside the tent door gives them soft water for washing. The water for drinking and cooking purposes they have to fetch from a farm a quarter of a mile away. The same farm supplies them with milk, butter, eggs and a Sunday or Saturday night chicken.

They give parties there nearly every week end. Their friends drive down to swim, lie on the beach and to broil steaks over the charcoal camp grill. The same handy waterproof chest holds some games and extra bathing suits.

When Sunday evening comes they simply stow everything away in the chest, lock it and drive it to the farmhouse where it is stored until they call for it the next week end.

Another couple who fully intend to own a place of their own in the country someday have made the first step toward this by buying a portable garage. They don't use it as a garage yet, however, but as a week-end camp. They have rented a view from a Connecticut hillside.

Here they have set up their week-end camp looking toward the view. Their friends come out and spend Sundays with them there.

Another couple asked for and got, as a wedding present, a trailer. They took their honeymoon in it, discovering Vermont. Later on they scouted around until they found a narrow lane running between two hayfields. A quarter of a mile down this the lane crossed a brook and there grew an old gnarled apple tree. The farmer who owned the land was glad to rent them the right to park their trailer there by the year. Every week end they drive out to their trailer. Inside it are all the things they need for camping out until Sunday night, including books, radio, golf clubs, fishing tackle. They have built a stone fireplace beside the brook where they do their cooking. They have fold-up canvas chairs, lots of cushions and those convenient roll-up mattresses I've already said so much about. They have picnic suppers there on moonlight nights and ask their friends to drive out from town to come to them.

## Picnics

PICNICS, to be really successful, require a few luxury touches. At least that's my feeling about them. Most people enjoy picnics more if they have a comfortable canvas chair (one of the fold-up ones which go easily into the trunk of the car) to sit on. And if there is some sort of table at which to eat or at least from which to serve the food. If you build your own picnic place you can set up a permanent table. If you're going picnicking in some strange place a low, folding camp table which you can take along in the car is a great help.

There are all sorts of elaborate, fitted picnic baskets, but just as good as these, I think, is any flat wicker basket with a hinged lid which can be securely fastened, into which to put unbreakable plates and cups, paper napkins, the picnic spoons, forks and knives, some paper towels and a pair of round wooden salt and pepper shakers.

Whatever else you may leave behind when you go on a picnic don't let it be the salt.

Picnic food depends on the locality where the picnic is to be. If you are going to picnic on the beach where you can have a fire and hang a pot over it why not have clam chowder? You can make the chowder at home and take it along in a big thermos jug. When you get to the beach

you will be able to buy fresh clams which can be cut up and added to the chowder and the whole mixture heated and simmered in a kettle over the fire while you take your swim.

A camp grill with charcoal to burn under it is a picnic convenience. Mutton chops are delicious broiled over the charcoal. So is a big juicy steak. Hamburgers are good picnic food. So are flapjacks.

The best picnics I know about are those which some friends of mine used to have at that lovely place, Islesboro, in Maine. We sailed across to an island where there is a stretch of perfect and lonely beach. There a big fire was built, and into the fire were put a number of carefully selected flat stones, one for each person. At the proper time, when the stones were heated through and through, each person was given a slice of steak to cook on his own flat stone. With the steak we had potatoes, roasted in the hot ashes of the fire, and roasted corn. Then a big covered jug filled with buckwheat batter was passed about. You poured enough for a cake on your hot stone which served as a griddle. Lots of fresh butter and lots of real maple syrup dressed the cakes to perfection.

# 10

# IF YOU HAVEN'T A HOME

## How to Make One

IF YOU HAVEN'T A HOME then the thing to do is to make one, at once, out of whatever you have.

That sounds like an Irish bull. But it's the soundest common sense.

A home isn't necessarily a whole house or even a part of one. It doesn't have to be an apartment or a hotel suite. It can be a single rented room. Or a trailer. Or a ship's cabin.

One young bride started her married life in a freight car drawn up on a railroad siding in the wildest part of Idaho. She had married a young engineer who had the job of building a new railway bridge. Between living in a hotel a hundred miles or so from where her husband's job was (and seeing him for a few hours every four or five days) and living right with him on the job she chose the latter. (Who wouldn't?)

When she arrived at the freight car her sole piece of household machinery was a Montgomery Ward catalogue. But she had ingenuity and a real flair for living. She looked over the inside of the freight car—it had two bunks built one above the other across one end and a cookstove and some shelves at the other—and then sat down on a pine stump beside the track, got out her catalogue and a pencil and went to work on her problem.

Ultimately (and in remarkably short time too) the freight car was transformed into what closely resembled a cottage in the Bavarian Alps.

The walls and ceilings were stained dark brown. The floor was covered with plain, all-color linoleum. This was bright lipstick red.

A good-sized closet was built between the wall and one end of the bunks. And a small window was cut into the wall at the opposite end. You could lie in bed and look out across a forest to snow-capped peaks.

This end of the car was separated from the rest by a wooden frame like a recessed peasant bed, which surrounded the bunks and which was painted bright blue. The opening to this was hung with curtains of red-and-white patchwork quilts. (These really were quilts which the bride cut into curtains.) They exactly matched the quilts on the bed and were looped back to show these and cost very little.

The wide doors of the freight car were fitted with glass sash, some of it hinged to form casements. A small serviceable door was cut into one side of the car down toward the end where the cookstove was, with a little ladder of steps.

A dresser was built on each side of the black stove and painted bright blue. The doors of the cupboards, like those of the clothes closet, were ornamented with bright decalcomania flowers. One dresser held books, the other blue and white and bright red plates and bowls. From big iron hooks fastened to a square sheet of copper and nailed to the wall hung several copper saucepans (bought with a wedding-present check), and long-handled spoons and forks.

In the center of the car stood an oak gate-legged table and four Windsor chairs of hickory. (The bride intended to use these in her house when she got a real one of her own.) And two big easy chairs (wedding presents), slip-covered in the same red-and-white patchwork as the curtains and bedspreads.

The bride was terribly proud of her home. (Do you wonder?) She sent snapshots of it to all her friends who had condoled with her for having to live in the wilderness. When spring came she sent for several gallons of white paint and a gallon of bright blue paint, and she and her husband had fun painting the outside of their car, themselves, all white with blue trimmings. They also made window boxes to go outside the big window and planted petunias—white and blue and rosy pink—in these. When frost came they filled the boxes with evergreens they dug up in the forest.

People from all over that country heard about the house and drove or rode down to see it. It wasn't at all unusual for a perfect stranger to arrive and say he'd come to see the "circus car." In that way the bride got to know lots of people.

When her husband's birthday came they decided to give a party and ask everyone they knew. The invitations, on postcards on which the engineer drew a pen-and-ink sketch of the circus car, requested each guest to bring his own knife, fork, spoon, plate and tin cup. But this did not keep anyone away.

It was a beautiful, clear, moonlighted night in early August. Rugs and cushions spread on the bank of the ravine gave everyone a place to sit. There was a huge log fire and music—a guitar and an accordion—singing and lots of stories. And for supper—hot, well-seasoned *paella* (rice stewed in olive oil with pieces of chicken, shrimps, red peppers, okra, chicken livers, garlic and herbs); crusty Italian bread, made by the baker of the bridge-construction gang; big, straw-covered flasks of chianti ordered from a California vineyard. And a birthday cake of rich devil's food, with a thick white icing and thirty-two white candles all aglow.

"And did you ever know such a wonderful party?" The bride sighed happily as she and her husband, hand in hand, waved good-by to the last guest riding away.

## Gypsies for Life

MANY OF THE VERY NICEST MEN in the world never stay put long anywhere. They hop about, looking at oil wells and emerald fields. If you're married to one of them and want to be a partner in his adventures and not just a frozen asset you've got to forego dreams of a snug little cottage under some sunny hill and learn to be a gypsy.

Gypsies aren't homeless folk. They simply carry their homes with them. The way the turtle does.

If you're to be a gypsy for life then why not do as the Romanies do? Have a carpenter make you two—or three—big, strong wooden crates. Have the lids made to screw down. And have the corners bound with metal strips. In one of these pack three or four big soft cushions and between the cushions four big colorful pictures with wide white mats and white wooden frames that you will enjoy living with wherever you are. So packed, and if they fit the crate, these will travel thousands of miles without cracking a glass.

Into the same crate can go a smaller box which holds a tea set, carefully packed (If you happen to own a silver one why store this away in a bank vault? Take it along and enjoy it.), and a lovely painted black tray, books, Kodak books, writing-desk equipment, breakfast tray and set.

On top there may be room for a soft, light-colored rug that you will enjoy having beside your sofa. Or several pairs of long, lovely colored damask or chintz curtains to be hung at your hotel-room windows.

The second crate could hold two or three good-sized lamps with their shades. Fit each lamp with at least ten feet of cord. You can never be sure where electric outlets will be. Some family photographs. Games. A very small radio—one of the new ones that have no wires at all and can go anywhere. A cocktail shaker and glasses. Some linen tea cloths and napkins. Have the cloths the right size for a square card table.

And six big candlewick bedspreads, white or cream color.

No, you are not going to start a lodging house. But those spreads will cover your hotel beds. And you can safety-pin others to cover a hotel sofa and overstuffed chairs into very passable and amazingly smart-looking slip covers.

They're easy to launder. And it's the work of a minute to unpin them and whisk them back into the crate when the time comes to break camp.

With this equipment (you'll probably think of a lot more things to add to this list) you can turn any hotel room into a *home*. Move the furniture around until the arrangement suits you and your way of living.

Take down the hotel pictures and hang your own. And your curtains. Buy some cheap glass vases and fill these with fresh flowers and greens. (It will be fun to choose these in the local markets.) Have the hotel give you a card table. Then you can ask the new friends you will make to have tea with you, really "at home." When you ask guests to dine with you at the hotel you can have them come upstairs first for cocktails which your husband will enjoy shaking up.

Not least of all, you can entertain your husband during the evenings in your own home.

## A Rolling Stone's Home

THAT'S WHAT MY FRIEND, who is a very clever and internationally famous journalist, calls herself. Her home is a large, light suitcase. It can be shipped by express or carried by a porter. It will stow away in an airplane.

In this my friend carries a bedcover made of a lovely rayon brocade in a very pale beige color. And four good-sized pillow covers of the same material. She has chosen this for its light weight, its neutral shade and its cheapness. Also it launders perfectly.

Also in the suitcase are two or three old flower prints, unframed but mounted on stiff white cardboard mats. And a pair of old Sandwich glass candlesticks, shaped like dolphins and pale sea green in color. A quaint old silver tea caddy, filled with Earl Grey Mixture. And two big chair covers of chintz with a cream-white ground and bunches of soft-toned flowers.

When the Rolling Stone arrives at a hotel anywhere she immediately asks to have the bed in her room replaced by one without any headboard or footboard. She also asks for four pillows. Ten minutes later her bed is covered with the rayon cover and the pillows are basted into the rayon slips and there is a lovely fresh-looking divan.

She has the pictures removed from her room and puts up her own flower prints (with thumbtacks she carries with her). Her toilet articles are all kept in the bathroom, and the top of the bureau becomes a sideboard with the Sandwich glass candlesticks, the tea caddy and a tea set she asks the hotel to furnish. She sends out for some flowers, safety-pins the chintz over the hotel armchairs, takes her typewriter out of its case and is completely "at home."

In this sort of room she can entertain fellow journalists. She can interview important people with more privacy and ease than in a hotel lounge. And she never succumbs to that homeless-cat feeling which overtakes most newspaper men and women who wander about the world without a fixed home.

She may be a rolling stone, but she carries her moss with her.

## If Your Home Is a Hotel

PERHAPS YOU'RE a businesswoman and live all the year round in a hotel. It's convenient and comfortable and inexpensive. And you have no housekeeping responsibilities.

But sometimes you do wish you had some place to entertain your friends beside the hotel lounge, restaurant or bar.

If you're a permanent guest in the hotel the management will probably be willing to paint or paper your room to suit you. (But how many people do this?) And why should you not start buying things for your own room that will give it character? After all, you'll probably have a real home someday. Ask the hotel to take out your bedstead and to give you a sofa bed. Then you will have a bed-sitting-room. Take the mirror off the bureau and hang this in the bathroom with a glass shelf under it for your toilet articles. The chest of drawers will still hold your clothing, but it won't have a bedroom look.

Take a tip from the nomads whose stories I've just told and work out some slip covers for the furniture. Think seriously about low end tables to flank your sofa. And several really good lamps. Glance again at Chapter Two and read again what I have said about the importance of lamps in a room.

Have only the pictures you like and select.

Get some material and make yourself curtains that really count for something decoratively.

Then when you've turned that bleak, cut-and-dried hotel bedroom into a bed-sitting-room which is distinctly your own invite your best beau to spend the evening playing Russian bank or backgammon.

You can serve beer and crackers and cheese. Or fruit and coffee made in an electric percolator.

You may want to get one of those little bars on wheels. At ordinary times it can be run into a corner of the room and have books and magazines on it.

And you may feel like investing thirty to forty dollars in an electric fireplace which you can set against a wall of your room with a clock and candlesticks on the mantel and two easy chairs beside it. After all, it is a good investment. You can always sell your electric fireplace secondhand and let it work its magic in some other woman's life, when you have your own home and its own lovely wood-burning fireplace.

## Entertaining in Public

WHEN YOU HAVE TO ENTERTAIN guests in a restaurant it's a great help if you can take them somewhere where you are known. You will have better service and more of an "at-home" feeling.

Hunt about the city until you find two or three restaurants you like. Naturally you'll choose ones that have comfortable tables set far enough apart to give you a degree of privacy. Look for quick, attentive service, good cooking, pretty china and table accessories.

If you choose restaurants that are *prix fixe* then you'll always know exactly what your party will cost.

You may want to select three—one very cheap, one moderate in price, and one expensive but superlatively good one. The last for very special occasions.

When you invite friends to lunch or to dinner or to Sunday-noon "brunch" at one of your restaurants it's a wise plan to telephone the restaurant ahead and reserve a table. If you're a regular patron they will see that you have the table of your choice. You can also ask for special table decorations of flowers or fruit if you wish. If you like you can order the menu in advance (and then there's none of that bother about choosing what to have that makes entertaining in public so much less spontaneous than entertaining in a home).

And if you've established credit you can sign the check after dinner (add fifteen per cent for service) without having to get out your purse and go into a business transaction in the presence of your guests.

If you choose restaurants that are famous for certain dishes your friends will enjoy being asked to try these.

And if you have already turned your hotel bedroom into a home you can take your guests back there after dinner to play bridge or other games, to listen to the radio or to talk comfortably.

## A Cocktail Party

YOU MAY WANT TO GIVE one of these for quite a large number of friends. If so you don't have to entertain them in the public bar.

If you live in a hotel you can always ask the management if there is a vacant suite or room which you can have for your party. The furniture can be moved out and a buffet table set up. You can ask for a radio to give you music for dancing during the party.

Don't forget lots of cigarettes and plenty of ash trays.

Don't forget fresh flowers and vases of greens.

It's the things like that that make for hospitality. You can add them to a bare hotel room and create an atmosphere which your guests will appreciate and remember with pleasure.


### HOW MISS A —— GOT A
### REPUTATION FOR SOPHISTICATION

Miss A—— lives at a women's club. It's convenient and economical, and her job keeps her so busy that she knows she would never have time to keep house, even if she had one to keep.

When Miss A—— wishes to entertain her women friends, college classmates who happen to be in the city, or those she used to know in the small town where she grew up, or women she has met through her job, she usually asks three of them to meet her at her club in time for a cocktail before dinner. They have this in the club lounge which is pleasantly furnished and cheerful. Then they go out to a small French restaurant Miss A—— has discovered a block away.

The proprietor of the restaurant is also the cook. And he cooks certain dishes superlatively well. Miss A—— always orders dinner in advance. The proprietor knows that she appreciates a red-and-white-checked tablecloth (as on the boulevards), crusty bread in a little basket on the table, fresh butter and a tiny bouquet of one red rose, a ring of white daisies and then a ring of blue cornflowers.

The menu never varies: soup *du jour*, served from a big tureen, coquille St Jacques, a mixture of fish and sauce and herbs baked brown in scallop shells, broiled chicken and mixed green salad, fine pears and a selection of cheeses. With the dinner they have a bottle of Graves Superieure. And later black, bitter after-dinner coffee.

This dinner costs Miss A—— eighty-five cents per person. With the wine extra. Say one dollar more. The cocktails at the club are thirty-five cents each.

It isn't an expensive evening, especially as after dinner Miss A—— brings her guests back to her club to talk or to listen to music or to play bridge. And it's usually a very successful one.

The out-of-town friends have the thrill of dining in an unusual foreign atmosphere (they think Miss A—— very dashing) with dishes they do not have at home. And always Miss A—— invites some woman to meet them who is an interesting personality.

Back in her home town Miss A—— has the reputation of being a wonderful hostess with a very cosmopolitan way of doing things. When she goes back to that town on a visit, which happens every year or two, her old friends give her a perfectly marvelous time.

## CASE HISTORY OF A YOUNG MAN WHO
## UNDERSTOOD WOMEN

Miss Jones was an only child and had always resented it. Also, she had never had a home. (Her mother was one of those women who are too happy in a hotel suite ever to leave it.)

"When I marry," Miss Jones used to say to herself, "I'm going to have a house big enough to take in all my friends at once."

Deliciously she thought of that big house as somewhere in the country. It would have lots and lots of windows, with crisp muslin curtains blowing in the breeze. And the front door would never be locked.

Not until long after she had fallen in love with Mr Snooks, and fully a week after she had promised to marry him, did it occur to Miss Jones that Mr Snooks's job downtown, to which he went early and from which he came home late, took a home in the country for them out of the range of possibility for years and years.

With the date for their wedding set Miss Jones and Mr Snooks went apartment hunting. The further they looked the longer grew Miss Jones's face. Usually it was a round, merry little face. But when Mr Snooks looked at it about four-thirty that afternoon, after three hours spent inspecting empty and minute bandboxes to rent for sums that threatened the prospective budget, it was decidedly despondent.

Mr Snooks was a man of resources. He hailed a taxi and took his lady for a drive in the park. In the course of that drive he found out how Miss Jones felt about anything that remotely resembled a hotel suite. And about the dream house that would have room in it for lots of friends and good times with them. Mr Snooks could understand this feeling because he was one of a big family and had been brought up in just such a house himself and loved it.

Right then and there this young couple gave up looking for apartments. Instead they answered the advertisements of "Lofts to Let." The one they finally rented, on a two-year lease, was the upper floor of a building which had once been someone's stable. The lower floor had been turned into a garage and an apartment for a chauffeur. The furnace which heated this also heated the big loft upstairs. This was really a beautiful room, with a beamed ceiling and wide windows at both ends. The rest of the loft they proposed to keep as one big room, whose walls and peaked and raftered ceiling they whitewashed a dead white. They painted the floor bright lipstick red and installed a big black shiny Franklin stove with large brass knobs, which would give them an open fire. The pipe led into the furnace flue. They spent all their money on lots of big, comfortable, low, upholstered furniture which they slip-covered in red-and-green-wool Tartan plaid. Two of the big divans made into full-sized twin beds at night. Some rough peasant emerald-green rugs were spotted on the red floor. Four low, sturdy end tables with very big black-and-gold plaster lamps had large black-and-gold marbleized shades. The effect was dramatic, gay and comfortable (bought on the installment plan from one of the leading department stores). However, each piece was selected with care and discrimination. The final touch was the addition of four huge oleander trees.

*They decided not to have a kitchen at all.* Instead of a kitchen they would have a bar, which would also combine the offices of a drugstore lunch counter. They built this boldly across one end of the room. Behind it were cupboards, one of which concealed an electric icebox and another a sink. The top of the cupboards was a shelf which ran along under the windows and held picturesquely some big red-and-brown casseroles, jugs and trays. Against the plaster wall at one side of the windows they hung copper saucepans where they were as decorative as they were handy for the electric stove, which was fitted cunningly into that end of the bar.

Inside the bar and under it, out of sight, were shelves for glass and china and for supplies like canned goods, seasonings and so forth. They set half a dozen high stools, cushioned in bright green leather, before the bar on the room side. Usually, however, meals are served on a table set up somewhere in the room.

The young Snooks are known among their friends as the most hospitable couple in their group. And their house is the most popular gathering place. Everyone else feels welcome. Everyone feels that having a party there is as much fun for Mr and Mrs Snooks as it is for the guests. And no more trouble. There's plenty of room for dancing, for charades, for trying new gymnastic exercises under a teacher. Last Christmas there was room enough for a *huge* Christmas tree and fifty of the Snooks's friends to gather round this and sing carols.

Mrs Snooks is a completely happy woman. She has everything she wants. (And we think more husbands should copy Mr Snooks.)

# 11

# ENTERTAINING YOUR HUSBAND

## Fun for Two

I KNOW ONE HUSBAND whose wife has entertained him successfully for twenty-two years. He lives in Washington, and he is a taxi driver.

I took his taxi one morning soon after I had started writing this book. It was a cold morning, but my driver was hatless and in his shirt sleeves. I asked him if he didn't feel cold.

He shook his head. "No, lady. You see I'm pretty fat." (He certainly was.) "That keeps me warm."

"Your wife must be a good cook," I said.

He swung round in the seat to give me his full confidence: "Yes, she is. She feeds me the best food in the world. She's a wonderful woman, my wife is. Would you like me to tell you how we met?"

I said I certainly would.

"Well, I met her at a party one Saturday night. And the next Wednesday we got married. That was twenty-two years ago now. And we've been laughing together ever since."

I don't know a better success story than that. After all, two people who have been laughing together for twenty-two years (and presumably are going right on laughing) have achieved something. Yes, that taxi driver's wife is really a *very* wonderful woman.

Let's analyze the secrets of that success:

1. She feeds him well.
2. She thinks of his comfort and tastes.
3. She amuses him.

## Feed the Brute

GOOD FOOD is always important. It seems as though you can't talk about entertaining without bringing food into the discussion over and over again. And by good food we mean, of course, food that is not only good *for* you, but food that you *like* to eat.

Many women don't think it matters very much what they eat when it isn't a party. Most men start their argument the other way round. They seldom can understand (or have much patience with) the fuss women will go to when they entertain. They argue that the food you serve to the family who belong and who are there all the time deserves more serious consideration than the food prepared for occasional guests.

If you're one of those who can be quite happy with just a cup of soup and a raw carrot to nibble when you dine alone don't expect your husband to share your views. Or your diet fads.

Start thinking of the meals you and he have together as *fun for two*. That is, think of them in terms of entertaining. Plan the menus as cleverly

(I don't mean extravagantly) as if this man who is going to eat them weren't your husband at all. At least *not yet*. Give him (and not incidentally, yourself) the fun of surprises in foods and in table decorations. Men do notice color schemes, though they usually don't say much about them.

One man who was facing very grave financial difficulties (he was threatened by the loss of the business he had spent half a lifetime to build up) all through one scorching-hot summer told his wife long afterward that what had helped him most through those trying months were the flowers she had on their breakfast table. She varied the bouquets and the vases for them from day to day so there was always freshness and variety. And she took pains to have cool-looking, white flowers with lots of green ferns on mornings when the thermometer was starting at eighty-five.

## The Comforts of Home

EVERYONE LIKES COMFORT, but men *demand* it.

Women frequently put up with uncomfortable furniture simply because they like its looks or because it is valuable. Or, silliest of all, because it seems too much trouble to change it. No man does that.

You have only to go into the clubs men plan for themselves and see the huge, deep, comfortable chairs and sofas, placed where the light is just right for reading, the big, practical tables for magazines and papers, the sturdy, small tables set just where you want one to hold your cigarettes or a glass of whisky and soda, the absence of dinky little objects to know how much a man values his creature comforts.

Your house is your husband's too. Naturally he wants to feel completely and comfortably at home in every room in it. He won't if there is just one room, tucked away in an odd corner, to be his "den." Every man wants a room downstairs to himself if the house is big enough for this. He needs a place where he can retire when he wants to concentrate on some piece of work and where his papers and books will not be disturbed. A house to be a home should reflect the various interests of all the members of the family in it.

But also he wants to feel at home in the living room and everywhere else in the house. If he doesn't he'll be dashing off to his office and to play golf.

Many living rooms are too feminine. (After all, most of them are decorated by women.) Often the furnishings women select seem to a man too fragile to be comfortable. Between creating for yourself a dainty, ultra-feminine background and having the kind of house your husband will look forward all day to coming home to what woman worth her salt (or her husband) doesn't choose the latter?

Men are usually annnoyed by clutter. They don't like dinginess either. (And quite right they are.) A priceless Duncan Phyfe chair that is uncomfortable to sit on and looks shabby has no charms for them. Men are usually quick to appreciate that well-groomed look we've talked about in an earlier chapter. They want it just as much in a house as in a woman.

They take these things for granted. They expect order and efficiency in a house just as much as they require it in an office. And they aren't in the least interested in the processes by which all this is brought about.

I'm sure my taxi driver's wife doesn't meet her husband when he comes home with tales of her difficulties with the kitchen stove or waxing the dining-room floor or with the butcher and grocer.

(And we hope you don't either.)

## Laughing Together

If SOMETHING really extraordinary or amusing (even if it's a joke on *you*) has happened to you during the day do you save it up to entertain your husband when he comes home?

Do you consciously (or unconsciously) collect little bits of information, anecdotes, side lights on character to share with him?

Do you think up things you can do together that will be different and *fun?*

The women men have always found most attractive have usually not been brilliant conversationalists or high-brow. They have been women with understanding of and really sincere liking for other people. And with a zest for living that kindles a responsive echo in everyone they meet.

I remember once being given a really terrifying side light on marriage. I was dining in a restaurant with a man, and he called my attention to a good-looking couple at a near-by table. "I know they're married," he said; "they haven't spoken one word to each other since they ordered dinner."

They were middle-aged people. They, too, might have been married for twenty-two years. But all too obviously they hadn't been "laughing together ever since."

## Hobbies for Two

Every MARRIAGE ought to be elastic enough to take in the private hobby of each partner. And still have room for several more hobbies which husband and wife can share.

Perhaps you can't stir up any great enthusiasm for your husband's stamp collection. Or for his cases of butterflies and moths. Or for the first editions he collects. He may be keenly interested in historical matters (while you can't even remember the date of your own birth). He may have a hankering to have a workshop in the cellar or in the garage to do carpentry. He may be interested in chemistry (though he's an advertising man or a banker). He may extravert his love for the sea by knowing all about and collecting ship models.

Or he may have no hobby at all and need one badly.

The finest thing about a hobby is that you can't do any pretending about it. You either like it or you don't. But you can balance your husband's carpenter's complex with a hobby of your own (this might be a study of the history of period architecture and furniture). It might be Early American glass or pewter or Lowestoft.

Then, following one of the universal laws of geometry, having two given angles, it's the simplest thing in the world to construct the third which has a relation to each of the other two.

A California woman whose husband was an amateur chemist got tired of hearing explosions and having horrible smells come from his laboratory which had been the laundry of their house. She was wiser than to object or complain. Instead she bought a book on perfumes. She read this herself and then left it lying about where her husband soon discovered it. He became enthusiastic about experimenting with synthetic flower scents. This was something his wife could be as interested in as he was. They played at this together and made perfumes which they gave to their friends, put up in bottles which the wife designed.

In fact, this hobby bolted clear away with them and ultimately became a business in which they are partners and very successful.

A man with one hobby is usually capable of taking on one or two more. The entertaining wife picks out a hobby she knows she will enjoy riding and trots it before her husband invitingly.

Presently both are well astride the hobby and galloping away together.

Everyone grows more interesting as he (and she) develops more interests. There was a man whose physician told him he must give up business altogether, though he was only fifty-two. He was appalled by the prospect of nothing to do for the rest of his life except to prowl about the house. (His wife was even more appalled.)

Then she made him a sporting proposition. She suggested that he draw up a contract with himself to take on one entirely new interest every year. At the end of the year he could drop it if he had exhausted its possibilities or found he really wasn't as interested in it as he had thought he might be. But he was bound by his contract with himself to keep it up for twelve months.

The idea appealed to him and he adopted it.

At sixty that man was so much more interesting and attractive (as well as much better in health) than he had been at fifty that his doctor was astounded. And his wife was as much in love with him as when he was forty.

Of the eight interests he had chosen—photography, minerology, gardening, modeling, chess, deep-sea fishing, eighteenth-century novelists and genealogy—he had abandoned only two—minerology and the novelists. His interest in gardening was something his wife could share. In fact, they designed and planted a garden together and she became an authority on growing rare lilies. (She actually wrote a book about this.)

Through the years they had both dreaded they actually had more fun together and entertained each other more than they had at any time since their marriage.

## Playing Together

IF YOU'RE MARRIED to a man who is keen about sports are there any of these (or even just one) that you play well too? If not, why not?

Perhaps you're embarrassed to appear as a beginner on the golf links or the tennis courts where your husband and his friends play really masterly games. But you can learn these games (and all the others) at a sports school in nearly every large city. Then you can surprise (and delight) your husband by letting him find you a darn good partner.

Even if you swim wouldn't you and your husband enjoy learning to swim to music, the new way this is being taught? What about going several times a week during the winter to skate at an ice rink where you can learn to imitate Sonja Henie? What about lessons in skiing? Or badminton? Or in the rhumba?

Your figure will be improved, and you and your husband will have a lot of amusing times doing these things. You'll make new friends through these interests. And the friends you already have will find you both a lot more fun to be with.

One young couple living in a city, and without much money to spend on fun, took up roller skating. They invited two other couples to do the same. One night a week the six meet at a public roller-skating rink, skate together for two hours and then go home to the apartment of one couple for sandwiches and beer and a game of poker.

If it's the present state of your figure which keeps you from appearing in a bathing suit or smart, tailored slacks or crisp linen shorts enroll at once in a reducing class. Six weeks' daily attendance at one of the really thorough courses will actually take off twenty pounds (sometimes more than that). When you catch a glimpse in the glass of your trim new figure you'll feel like dashing right out and buying the prettiest bathing suit you can find and diving into a pool right away.

Don't wait for your husband to make the discouraging discovery that his wife isn't as much fun to be with as when you and he were first married. Don't let middle-aged slump or the Will to Be Dreary deprive you of a companionship that can (and should) entertain you both as long as it exists. Do something about it. And right *now*.

You can:

1. Look up the schools which teach sports and find out about classes, private lessons, hours and terms.
2. Send for booklets on trips you can take (most inexpensively) on tramp freight boats. Lay this before your husband and suggest that you and he run away on such a cruise. When he sees how little it costs he will read further and further. And when he starts thinking about the adventure of putting in at half a dozen picturesque ports on strange coasts he won't be able to resist the impulse you have given him.
3. Get a good road map and pick out some beautiful places within two days' driving distance that you and he can go to over a long week end. Start discovering America and your own and neighboring states. Take a Kodak (or a movie camera) with you, and reel as you go.
4. If he (and you) used to love canoeing you could give each other a joint Christmas present of a collapsible canvas boat in which to take trips together down some of the small rivers. You can put up at country hotels along the stream of your choice or, what is even more fun, carry a camp kit and camp out. Either way you'll have adventures.
5. If you haven't a car you can go by bus to some point from which you

can take a week end (or longer) walking trip. This is much better for the figure than riding all day on rubber tires. And it can be a lot of fun.

## Running Away Together

ONE MARRIED COUPLE who happen to be very good friends of mine are determined not to let the fact that they are parents of three children they simply adore cramp their style as husband and wife.

So every so often they run away together.

They have two or three pet places they run off to. In summer they're apt to take a train out to a tiny village near the tip of Long Island which they discovered years ago and which they never tell anyone about for fear it will become popular.

They leave their bag at the village hotel, go to the general store for a beefsteak, rolls, butter, cheese and beer. They carry these and the folding camp grill they take with them out to a strip of sandy beach which no one (so far) seems to have discovered. They collect driftwood and build a fire. While it burns they bathe in the surf and lie on the sand and bathe again. They run races and play tag and forget that they are the parents of three rapidly growing up young people. Then they broil their steak and have their picnic meal and wait for the moon to come up, snuggled under the warm rug they have brought with them.

They laugh and tell each other confidences and have a really wonderful time just by themselves. Not once do they mention the children or domestic problems or any of the details of the life they have run away from.

All their friends consider that they have a highly successful marriage. And each one of them knows that he (and she) is married to the most entertaining person in the whole world.

## Evenings at Home

EVERY MARRIAGE has a lot of these in the course of every year of it. Are yours going to be dreary and full of yawns? Or are you and your husband going to look forward to a quiet evening just by yourselves, by the fire or on the porch, after the children have gone to bed?

These are the times for the talks about the books and magazine articles you both read. For music together. Perhaps your husband has always had a secret belief (like the Irishman) that though he never *has* played the violin he guesses he could. And maybe he can.

Cribbage and chess and Chinese checkers and dominoes are fun for two. You can keep your scores for a month and see to it that the loser gives the winner a party.

After a couple of hours' play it's fun to explore the icebox and have a supper before you go upstairs. Or carry the supper up on two trays and have it luxuriously in bed.

## The Dream Husband

HE IS THE MAN who writes his wife a little note once in a while not to tell her to have something fixed on the car or to telephone the plumber about the roof. But to tell her that he loves her and she's the most adorable woman in the world.

He is the man who rings up from the office once in a while and asks his wife if she wouldn't like to go out somewhere for dinner together that evening. And when she says, "I'd love it," sends her a flower to wear and comes home early enough to dress and take her out with the same gay anticipation they had during their engagement days.

He is the man who always goes ahead when they go to a restaurant together, who goes up to the headwaiter and sees that they have the table they want and who takes the initiative when it comes to ordering the dinner. He doesn't just leave this to his wife (she has enough of ordering meals at home).

He is the man who is prompt and masterful with doormen and taxi drivers. He never keeps you standing in the rain when you come out of a theater or a night club. Instead he dashes out and returns with a taxi in which you drive off *ahead* of the crowd.

He is the man every woman longs to be married to.

He is the man every woman *can* be married to if she is really determined to preserve the romance and the glamour that shone so radiantly over the first days of their life together.

For, there's no getting around it, this is *her* job. So far there's nothing about "entertaining your husband" in the vows of the marriage service. But don't you think there ought to be?

# 12

# HAVE YOU THE FRIENDS YOU WANT?

## You Can, You Know

IF YOU HAPPEN TO HAVE what I call a "flair for living" then it doesn't matter how many friends you have or how devoted you are to them. You always have room for more.

Your life may be as full of interest as a fruitcake is of plums, but if you have a genuine, deep-seated zest for living life to the full then you are always eager to make it richer, plummier.

Life has a way of responding to this sort of demand. It gives those people who have an appetite for living, who welcome friends, interests, enthusiasms, fun, *what they want.*

Where you happen to live has nothing to do with it. A husband and wife living on a lonely ranch in the Far West seemed far removed from friends and opportunities for making new ones. Until a doctor from an Eastern city met the ranchman, realized the man's quiet strength and the fineness of his character and later wrote him to ask if he would take as a boarder on his ranch a millionaire patient of his who had had a nervous breakdown.

The sick man made such a marvelous recovery and came back to New York so enthusiastic about the ranch and its owners that presently they were besieged by people wanting to come and stay with them.

Quite a number of well-known, famous and really interesting men and women have gone there to stay. And when the ranchman and his wife come on to New York or to Washington they have a host of warm friends eager to make them welcome and to give them a good time.

## If There's a Will

THE ONLY REAL, fundamental difference between individuals and what makes one person different from another isn't in what each one *has* or in their mental gifts and talents. It's the amount of will each one has to develop and make the most of himself.

Darwin announced this theory, and William James seconded it. So you can take it on their authority, not just on mine.

If you have the will to make yourself the kind of person others find interesting, someone people enjoy being with, you'll have all the friends you want. And all your life. It won't matter at all where you live or how much (or how little) money you have or the size or kind of house you live in. Of course if you're this kind of person you couldn't possibly have a drab, dreary house. You'd just have to do something about it. And you would too.

You won't even have to think about being hospitable and what to do to make your friends feel at home whenever you ask them to the house.

They'll all be so thrilled to be asked and so eager to come and find it so much fun being with you that your party will go over with a bang without your ever being really aware what you did to make it go.

There was a period (some writers have nicknamed it the Gilt and Tinsel Era) about forty years ago when very rich hostesses vied with each other to give grander and more elaborate parties. They spent enormous sums on floral decorations and stage effects, on the food they had at them and on the clothes they wore to them. They engaged highly paid entertainers—occasionally an entire theatrical company to give a special performance of a popular musical comedy—to entertain their guests.

To read about those times today seems unreal. What was the matter with the people themselves that their friends didn't find them fun to be with, without the dancers and the tenor soloists and the professional clowns? What was the matter with the friends who were asked to these parties that they couldn't amuse and entertain each other?

Really nothing was the matter with these people except that they didn't develop themselves to be interested *in* (and therefore interesting *to*) others. They never gave their natural flair for living a real chance. And so they missed a lot of fun that our generation which lives so much more simply and which would always rather do a thing themselves than sit on a gilt chair and watch someone else do it (even better) has all the time.

Yes, we've advanced a long way since the Gilt and Tinsel Decade, and we're still going places. How do I know this? Simply because practically every single person I know, young and old, is learning something new, doing something different from what they did a year or even six months ago. They are taking stock of themselves (liabilities as well as assets) and are out to make the most of themselves and of all their opportunities.

What's the result? All of them are more alive and therefore more attractive than they were before they started on their self-development campaign. All of them seem to have more friends and to appreciate and enjoy the friends they have.

All of them, so they tell me, are getting more fun out of life.

## There Are Ways

IN OUR LAST CHAPTER we discussed a number of ways in which any woman can make life more entertaining for her husband and herself. Many of the suggestions given there apply equally to this matter of making more friends.

When you go on a trip, anywhere, you inevitably meet new people. Some of these may not be very interesting to you (or you to them), but by the well-recognized law of averages there are sure to be at least one or two who are your kind and whom you will enjoy having for friends.

But don't expect to have them walk up to you and make all the friendly advances. You have to meet them halfway. This starts with a pleasantly expectant attitude toward your adventure and the people you are going to meet in the course of it. Just that point of view has magic in it. If you can *believe* that you are going to have a good time and meet some people you will enjoy and if you really do welcome those you find, you will find them. In Tahiti, in Texas or in New York.

If you join a class to learn tap dancing or backgammon or astrology or high-diving stunts you will meet new people who have been drawn to that class by the same interest that takes you to it. There's nothing like an enthusiasm or a hobby shared for making friends. Don't expect to feel drawn to *every* member in the class. Remember the law of averages. But even one new friend whom you find really companionable, plus what you get from the class, repays you for the effort and the time you give to it.

Today there's no reason in the world why anyone, living anywhere in this country, shouldn't be enjoying the fun and getting the stimulus of learning something new.

There are schools of adult education (no, don't be scared off by that alarming term) in every city of any pretensions to size. You will find them in the up-and-coming smaller cities, too, under various names and directed by various local organizations. Even the suburban communities frequently have them.

These schools offer courses in a bewildering array of subjects, from writing for radio to golf and ancient Arabic. You can satisfy your long-felt longing to find out about costume designing as a career. You can peep into the secrets of counterpoint. Or learn all about Early American quilts. You have only to inquire about them at the nearest public library or at the superintendent's office of the high school. Or from the local women's club, or the Chamber of Commerce or the Y.W.C.A.

Since you want to increase the number of your friends (as well as your knowledge of French, botany, current events and bridge) you'll probably find a class more fun than taking private lessons. Even if you are dead-set on culture a class in which you have the stimulus of competition with others is often a worth-while spur to enthusiasm when this begins to lag.

And if there really are no schools near enough for you to go to regularly there are correspondence courses, offered by many of the state universities as well as by commercial schools. Many of these are very, very good. (Those offered by the School of Adult Education of Columbia University are famous.) Even this sort of study opens doors for one into adventures later on.

## Is It Chance?

THERE SEEMS TO BE A LAW that when you become really very much interested in a subject or an idea or a place and do what you can to increase and satisfy that interest the opportunity to know more about it comes to you.

A woman, living in a really very dull little town in the Midwest and tied there by family ties and very little money, wanted desperately to travel. Some part of her nature languished for want of warm, sun-bright colorful countries and people in picturesque costume carrying on a life that was strikingly different from any life she had known.

Wisely she decided not to frustrate that entirely right and natural desire. She could not sail away to Peru as she longed to do, but she could send to the steamship companies for folders about trips there. She could read all the books about Peru in the town's library and then write for more books on the subject from her state library. In a year and a half that woman was thoroughly "up" on Peru and her interest in the country was known to nearly everyone in the town. So it was quite natural that the wife of the bank president should ring her up one day to say that her husband was bringing a stranger home to dinner and that this stranger (another banker) had spent years in Peru and please wouldn't our heroine come to dine to meet him and to entertain him on her favorite subject. Nor did it end there. The banker made it possible for the woman and her husband to take a two months' trip to Peru where they were entertained by the most interesting people and had exactly the kind of time the woman had dreamed of having.

That is just one example of how this law works, but I feel sure if you think over your own life you will remember several times when this sort of thing happened to you. It seemed like chance. But was it?

Why not deliberately make use of that law of like attracting like and draw to yourself people who have the same interests that you have?

## Pets

PETS OF EVERY SORT (even tropical fish) have been known to bring people together and to start lifelong friendships. And even romances.

A lonely woman who really loved birds started to raise canaries for her own pleasure. All she had was a two-room apartment too. For some time those two rooms housed herself and twenty-three canaries! She read up on breeds and types and songs (and everything else there is to know about a canary). Gradually she got into correspondence with other canary fanciers in other parts of the country, among them a professor of ornithology in a Southern college. He enjoyed the correspondence so much (presumably they wrote about more than just canaries) that he came North during one vacation just to see her. And when he went back he took her with him, as his wife.

Another woman, living in a small (and, alas! dreary hotel) in New York and not knowing anyone in the city, in desperation went down to the Bide-A-Wee Home for stray animals and asked for a dog. She chose an impudent-looking Irish terrier, one of those dogs everybody simply feels obliged to smile at. By the time she'd had him a week and taken him on daily walks in the park she had talked with more people than she used to talk to in a month.

Ultimately she came to know another woman, also living in a hotel and lonely, who loved dogs. And soon after that the two decided to take an apartment together and give Michael O'Flaherty a real home.

## Read, Look, Listen

HERE ARE some very practical suggestions (you know by this time that I'm all for being practical) for ways to make yourself not only a well-informed person about the world you live in but how to have fun while improving yourself.

The list, as I have made it, will keep you (and me) busy for a whole month.

Repeat next month and thereafter in monthly doses and see what it accomplished for you:

1. *Read* one good daily newspaper every day. Read it thoroughly. Don't stop at the headlines.
2. *Read* one weekly magazine which gives you a review of the news (*Time, Life, Newsweek,* etc.).
3. *Read* one monthly magazine of general information (*Reader's Digest,* for first choice).
4. *Read* one magazine on personal psychology which will help you to understand yourself and others and will show you how to get more out of life. (*Your Life* is one. And there are others.)
5. *Read* one current novel and one non-fiction book about which people are talking.

6. *See* one really good motion picture every month.
7. *See* one play. (If you live in a city with a theater. If you don't at least read the drama news and stage criticisms in your daily newspaper and in your weekly news review. Then when you go to a city where there are theaters you will know which plays you will enjoy seeing.)
8. *Hear* one fine concert. By radio if that is the only way you can do so.

So far we haven't said anything about your husband in this campaign for self-improvement. Don't leave him behind. After all, why not be partners in *that* as much as in everything that isn't so pleasant and thrilling?

If you live in a suburb of a large city why not propose to your husband that you and he "do" a matinee one Saturday in every month? You'd find it fun to meet him in town in time to lunch together, going to a different restaurant each time, and then go to see a play and have a cocktail in some amusing place before you dash for your train.

And it isn't such a great stretch of imagination to see that sometimes you *won't* dash right away for the train. Instead you'll stay on and dance together somewhere and have a really festive time. And take a quite late train home.

## Newcomers in Town

EVERYONE, when she first moves into a new community, wonders a little how she is going to make friends there. We're all apt to forget that, as newcomers, we are just as interesting to the neighbors as we find them.

They're just waiting, some of them on tiptoe, for a sign of friendliness, at which they'll come and call and ask you to do things with them.

Americans are the friendliest people on earth. Most American towns are hospitable to newcomers. The ministers of the various churches always make calls on new families. Often, too, they ask some of their parishioners to call. The children of the family will soon make friends at school, and naturally the parents of those friends of theirs will want to know you and your husband.

There's nothing difficult about it at all really. Only, again, you can't wear a standoffish and hard-to-know expression and attitude and expect people not to believe you mean it. You can't put up hurdles and expect strangers to leap them to get to you.

So clear the course. Don't be afraid of strangers (or of yourself). Realize that you really are a delightful person to know. Remember that law we talked about just now, and draw to you the friends you want to have.

## Clubs

OF COURSE this is just what most clubs are for. They provide a place and occasions for people who like the same things and each other to get together.

But, of course, there are clubs and clubs. Some can be pretty dreary, a sort of catchall of unwanted personalities. But others really are fun. The best, of course, include men and women in their membership.

If you can why not belong to at least two clubs, one which will bring you into touch with other women who happen to be interested in some interest you have, like bridge or gardens or current events or house decoration. And one in which you will meet men and have the fun of discussions with them or of playing games with them.

Don't join a garden club and expect to meet anything but dozens of other women. And you aren't apt to gather up an exciting new beau at a women's bridge club either. But you will make women friends there. And you'll improve your game. And being a good bridge player is decidedly an asset when you take that cruise you're planning to go on soon. Also, it will make you a most desirable week-end guest in many households.

But you can join a political club in your locality. (Join it fully prepared to do some work.) You'll meet more men there than women. Get really interested in the community where you live. That interest will warm other people's interest in you and make them want to know you and to ask you to their houses.

If you have a hobby then inquire about a club which is built around this. If you haven't a hobby get one. And then find the club which will bring you in touch with others who are as enthusiastic as you may be about roller skating or skiing, hiking, music or sketching.

We can't guarantee the same result that overtook the lady who raised canaries, but we do guarantee that if you truly want to make more friends and show yourself to be a friendly sort of person others in the group will meet you at least halfway.

## As Others See You

ALL OF US TODAY are self-conscious in a way people of a generation or two ago weren't. People today believe in facing themselves and in checking up their personal assets and liabilities, the way a businessman takes stock of his business at least once a year.

Few of us can do this for ourselves. It's almost impossible to be sufficiently impersonal to see oneself objectively. But there are professional analysts (I don't necessarily mean those with "psycho" attached to the name, though I heartily approve of them too) who will do this for you and for an amazingly moderate fee.

There have been articles in the magazines recently by women who have put themselves through this checkup which tell what they got from it and how it started them on a new path of self-development. (I remember one in the *Reader's Digest* particularly.) A really thorough diagnosis will give you a knowledge of yourself as others see you. You can find out how your manner during an interview, your voice, your ability to converse interestingly, your choice and use of English, your way of wearing your clothes, your taste in accessories (gloves, handbag, handkerchief, etc.), the way you wear your hair, your walk, posture and make-up impress a perfect stranger.

And you will be given suggestions for improving yourself where you need improvement. You will be put in the way of lessons in posture and how to put on powder and *keep it on*. You can learn from a professional what colors and what style of dressing is most becoming to you. Most of us don't know this until we are taught.

If you're overweight (all over or just in spots) you can find out about a reducing diet or a class where your figure will be remodeled scientifically.

If there's a new way you could do your hair, which would actually make you look ten years younger and much smarter, wouldn't you be glad to know about it? And wouldn't you dash right over to the place and have it done that way and then try the effect on your husband or your best beau *at once?*

Of course. Any woman would.

We Americans believe in success. And we believe, what is more, that success is waiting for everyone who will go after it. Success in business or in a profession or in one of the arts isn't really as important as success in the greatest of all arts, the art of living. If you can improve your chances of success by going to a "success school" (you can even do this by correspondence too) and by *repackaging* yourself—actually that is just what it is—isn't it up to you to do it?

## That Will to Be Dreary Again

WHAT keeps you back?

Why don't you do these things and not just read about doing them?

Why don't you take that hint from Darwin and William James I gave you a little while back and exercise your will to make the most of yourself?

There's only one reason why you don't. It's that miserable little Will to Be Dreary getting in its work on you again. It's determined to turn you into a defeatist if it can. It challenges you constantly to exert all your Will To Live to overthrow it.

You can't afford to let up on it a single day of your life.

There was once a woman (I leave you to guess her name) who thought she knew all about the Will to Be Dreary. She even attempted to write about it to warn others how it sneaks in and tries to keep them from making living fun.

This woman was asked to go to a party (it was in Washington, a city she really adores) to be given by some dear friends of hers for their debutante daughter. She knew it would be a lovely party and she would meet a lot of old friends there and would have a perfectly lovely time. So she said she would go. And her friend, who was giving the party, engaged a room for her at a hotel and wired back how terribly glad she was she could come.

The woman looked forward for a week to the party. Then on the day before she woke up and thought: "Goodness, how tired I am! And that dress I was going to wear isn't right. It bulges where no dress should bulge. And it's an awful waste of time (and money) to dash down to Washington just to go to *one* party and come right back the next day. And I'll be even more tired when I get back. And I probably won't meet anyone very interesting or exciting at the party. And Laura (the hostess) will be much too rushed to give me more than a word. And I don't believe it's worth the effort. And I'm *not going.* . . ."

And she sent a wire to her hostess that she was sorry but all her plans were changed and she couldn't go.

Yes, she did just that. Though she knew her friend really wanted her to come. And counted on her. And had gone to the trouble to engage a room for her at the hotel.

Then, just about the time when she would have been taking the train to Washington, she went for a walk. And she met another friend, and as they walked along she told her how she had been going out of town to a party and had decided not to go. The friend turned and looked at her. She said:

"Humph, same old Will to Be Dreary, I see. It just sneaked up on you and wouldn't let you have fun."

The more the woman thought about it the more she knew this was right. And the more ashamed she felt. And the more determined to show that impish little Will to Be Dreary that she, and not he, was running things in her life.

She went into the nearest Western Union office and wired her friend that her plans had been changed at the last minute and she *was* coming, after all. Then she went home, packed, called up the Airways office and caught the first plane to Washington.

On the plane she ran into a Nice Man she hadn't seen for months (he was going to the party too). They had tea together at an altitude of four thousand feet. And when it was time for the dinner he came round to her hotel and took her to it.

The party was really as lovely as she had known, long ago, it was sure to be. There were lots and lots of her old friends there and they all seemed terribly glad to see her. And she picked up a brand new beau and danced until four in the morning and enjoyed every single minute of it.

And dashing for her train back to New York the next morning (she felt better after three hours' sleep than she'd felt for weeks), she took a taxi whose driver gave her just the story she wanted for the book she was writing.

After which I leave it to you to decide whether or not it was worth while to overcome the Will to Be Dreary and show him who is the dictator of somebody's life.


## CASE HISTORY OF A CITY MOUSE WHO DISCOVERED COUNTRY MICE LIKED HER CHEESE

Louise B—— has a terribly exciting job with a big shop in San Francisco. She lives in a four-room apartment on Telegraph Hill, with a wide balcony which hangs over the bay. It is the first home of her own she ever had and she had the best time of her life decorating it to suit herself.

Every room in it fairly sings with color. Everything in it is chosen for comfort and refreshment of body and mind to dramatize the breathtaking view of hills and sea.

It's no wonder Miss B—— hates to leave it, even for a week end with friends at Burlingame.

Miss B—— is bright and amusing and more than average good-looking. She is much in demand as a week-end guest. But Miss B—— is also a person. She doesn't want to be guest every week end. She wants to be hostess herself sometimes.

During the week from Monday to Friday her job keeps her too busy to do much entertaining. For this reason Miss B—— concentrates her attention on week ends. Every two or three weeks she asks a friend, or a friend and her husband, to spend the week end with her *in the city*. And she doesn't always ask friends who live out of San Francisco either. Occasionally she asks a friend who lives in the city but who enjoys going away from her own home and being a guest, even in the same town.

Miss B—— goes in for luxury touches in her entertainment. Really lovely bedroom fittings for the guest. (The guest room also overlooks the bay.) The service of a part-time maid to unpack the guest's bag when she arrives and who comes in to pack her when she leaves. A breakfast tray so pretty that it almost distracts attention from the things on it— chilled orange juice, hot popovers and sweet butter and orange-blossom honey, coffee to make you sigh with delight.

Many of Miss B——'s friends are married and live in small houses and have lots of small children and not a great deal of money. Consequently at home they do not have all of these luxury touches. They appreciate them all the more when they week-end with Miss B——.

For amusement Miss B—— offers her guests all the sights of the city. Sometimes they *do* a museum or inspect the gardens in Sunset Park. Sometimes they take bus rides. Miss B—— plans ahead for concerts, really interesting lectures and theaters. Usually, if the guest comes on Friday, they have the first dinner at home on the balcony, and Miss B—— will have asked one or two of her men friends to drop in after dinner to spend the evening talking, singing or playing bridge. On Saturday evening Miss B—— takes her guests (and frequently two other friends) to dinner at a restaurant (San Francisco's restaurants are famous the world over). On Sunday there's a very late breakfast, about noon, to which other people, who know Miss B—— is entertaining, drop in. After this there is the rest of the day for amusement until a hot supper (which may be sent in from a restaurant near by) about seven-thirty.

None of her friends ever pity Miss B—— for spending week ends in town. A number of them who have country homes look forward to the fun they know they are going to have when the city mouse shares her cheese with them.

# 13

# WHAT TO BUY FOR ENTERTAINING

## If You're a Bride

You MAY BE MAKING PLANS for your wedding and for your first home of your very own. In that case part of those plans will take in the friends you and that attractive young husband of yours are going to want to ask to the house.

Marriage is truly a partnership of two. But those two people have relationships stretching out on all sides of them (like the threads of a spider's web). And the stability of the partnership, as well as its success, frequently depends a lot on the way those threads are fastened to outside supports. And how far they stretch out.

Planning for friends in your married life means planning for companionships which actually strengthen your marriage and help to keep it in sound working order. It doesn't mean that you don't consider your relationship to your husband the most important thing in your life. It *does* mean that you want to make your life big enough for that relationship to grow in.

## What Would You Like for a Present?

THIS IS THE ONE TIME in your life probably when you'll have that question asked you any number of times.

Don't look shy and hang your head and murmur, "Oh, anything." In the first place this isn't true. Who wants fourteen sets of peppers and salts? Or six salad bowls and not a single breakfast-tray set? Your friends really do want to give you what you want and can use and not something to be poked away on the top shelf of some closet until it seems to you safe to give it away. Or to send it to a Jumble Sale.

Speak right up, and firmly. Now is your chance, and it may never come again. Get out the list of furnishings that you will need for your house and look it over. Aunt Mary has offered to give you flat silver. And your husband's older brother has written that his present is to be a rug for your living room. If he is married and knows about houses and the way women feel about them he'll send you a check and let you choose the rug yourself.

"But," you tell the friend who has asked you that promising question, "I'd love an electric heater to go on the sideboard and keep things hot when we have a buffet meal." (She can get one for as little as $8.00). Or, "I'd like a tall 'butler's tray' which can stand in the living room and hold the drinks when we have a party." This need not cost more than $10. Or, "I'd simply *adore* a big brass knocker for the front door."

Here are some suggestions for your list. Naturally I have not put down the things you will want for your house when you are not entertaining and which will make it really livable. But here are some of the things that will help you as a hostess and will make entertaining *fun* for you and for your guests.

## For Hall and Living Room

A good hall mirror.

A good-looking umbrella stand, big enough to hold your friends' dripping umbrellas as well as those belonging to the family.

A fold-up coat rack. One of those which can be pushed back into a single upright and kept like that on ordinary occasions. But it is susceptible to being pulled out to hold as many as twenty coats on hangers when you are having a party.

Two dozen plain, substantial coat hangers. Those made of Luxite are the best for all purposes. A gadget which can be fastened to the inside of the door of your hall closet to hold ten or a dozen hats without crushing.

(This and the coat rack are great helps when you are entertaining a good many people and you don't want to have to take your guests upstairs to leave their coats and hats. The coat rack costs approximately $20 and the hat rack approximately $12.)

A great big canvas umbrella, useful to hold over people getting in and out of cars at your door on a rainy day. Like one of those doormen have. Or a golf umbrella.

A high "butler's tray."

A big metal bell, with a lovely tone, to call people in from the garden for games or meals or telephone calls.

A Servidor bar to attach to the closet door.

## For the Living Room

At least six big, smart-looking, clear-glass ash trays.

Glass boxes for cigarettes.

Glass coasters to go under highball glasses to protect your table tops.

A good-sized, low, round, folding tea table. Beware of wobbly ones. Choose one that is really strong and doesn't threaten to tumble over if anyone bumps into a leg.

A wheeled cart to bring in tea things and other drinks.

A "curate's assistant."

A long, low coffee table to stand in front of your sofa all the time. This is for your everyday use, of course, but it's practically indispensable when you have guests. The top of the table should be level with the seat of the sofa. And it should be more than one half as long as the sofa. Most coffee tables are too small and too teetery.

A number of tea cloths to fit your tea table, and lots of dainty, tiny tea napkins.

Big, clear glass vases for rhododendron leaves and other greens.

A pair of candelabra. To stand on the piano or on the buffet table when you entertain.

Four matching silver candlesticks. Or four clear-glass ones for your dinner table.

A charming tea set. If Aunt Mary is going to present you with all the flat silver you will need perhaps Aunt Martha and Uncle George will give you a silver tea set. Perhaps Aunt Martha may have a "family one" which she doesn't use and which she would pass on to you, the bride of the family. But if no one gives you a silver one then get a tea set of some lovely, fine china that you will enjoy using. Or one of some simple but colorful pottery.

"Nests" of small tables. Get out the saw at once and follow directions for cutting down their legs.

A dozen folding chairs (more if you intend to give large bridge parties or to entertain your political club).

Several folding card tables. And *strong* ones.

A portable radio. There will be times when you want to have a friend for tea out in the garden and neither of you wants to miss an important news broadcast.

## For the Dining Room

A big coffee urn, chromium plated.

An electric food heater. Of course you can get very grand ones of chromium or copper which cost more than $25. But also you can get one for as little as $8.00, which will keep two big casseroles piping hot during a protracted buffet meal.

Several huge clay casseroles. The kind the French peasants use for their cooking are picturesque enough to stand on your buffet table. Even very big ones need not cost more than $3.50.

Two cocktail shakers, a big one and a medium-sized one. The things most people give to brides are only just big enough for two. Romantic and practical when you and he are all by yourselves. But you're rather up against it when you have guests.

A double bowl to hold cracked ice with an inner container for stewed fruit, or yoghurt, or fresh raspberries; or even for caviar when you are making a Gesture.

Four or six big plates to hold hors d'oeuvres. The plates should be exactly alike.

Several dozen very small knives with bright-colored composition handles. For fruit or to spread butter and jam when you serve these at tea.

Two big wooden salad bowls.

Wooden plates for salad. Or little individual bowls.

Individual covered bowls of colorful pottery to hold oyster stew or black bean or French onion soup when you serve these for guests.

A chafing dish.

A Toastmaster.

Big brandy glasses.

Glass, china, linen ad lib. (but the right sizes and colors).

## For the Kitchen

An electric Mix-Master.

An electric fruit juicer.

An electric ice-cream freezer.

Several copper saucepans with covers which can be used to cook in and to serve from.

## For Porch, Terrace and Garden

A picturesque bar wagon.

Tall hurricane lamps. These come with a place at their base to hold flowers.

An outdoors dining table. Of iron, with a glass top. Or a real kitchen table painted a bright color and with the top covered with pretty oilcloth.

Chairs of the right height to go with the table. Be sure they are comfortable.

Amusing tablecloths and napkins to match.

Amusing, gay, colorful china.

Knives and forks with colorful composition handles.

Two big jars or pots to hold little trees or greens.

Games: croquet, quoits, archery, deck tennis, ping-pong, badminton.

## For the Guest's Bedroom and Bath

A folding trunk rack.

A breakfast tray with legs.

A china breakfast set.

Two dozen coat hangers.

A small folding ironing board, and a small-sized electric iron.

A bedside radio.

Really smart writing paper and envelopes.

Good lamps.

Lovely sheets, blankets, comforter and chaise-longue cover.

## The Entertaining Closet

No, I DON'T MEAN ONE that does tricks when you open the door. The name refers to the closet or cupboard, anywhere in the house, where you store away all the things you use for parties. One woman living in a small but cleverly compact New York apartment had a cupboard built into her front hall with shelves to hold the china, glass, linen and silver (triple plate) which she uses whenever she entertains. Giving a party, even a buffet meal for thirty or forty people, in her big studio doesn't mean upsetting her tiny kitchenette. And when she isn't giving a party her kitchenette is never crowded with large-size casseroles, platters and piles of dinner plates and cups and saucers.

If your house is low on closet space then consider educating your husband (and yourself) to carry your raincoats, galoshes, walking sticks and umbrellas upstairs and leaving the hall closet in which to store away the folding chairs, card tables, picnic basket, paper napkins and table-cloths and china and glass you use for entertaining.

You could have a Servidor fitted to the inside of the hall-closet door. When you give a big party, and the closet is empty of its party equipment, you can fit the shelf of the Servidor as a dressing table and turn the closet into a useful "powdering room" for the women guests.

Or if your apartment is pocket-handkerchief size a Servidor on the hall-closet door can be used as a bar when you have a party.

## Emergency Rations

EVERY WOMAN who keeps house has discovered a number of canned, bottled or packaged foods that are useful to have on hand when guests arrive unexpectedly, or a party runs on and on, or when more guests come than you have prepared for.

Every woman has her own pet tricks for these emergencies. Have you ever met an influx of four unexpected guests by sautéing a finely chopped onion in butter and turning a cup of rice into this until the grains have absorbed all of it? Then turn the warmed, buttery rice into a casserole, pour over it a can of consommé or chicken soup and place this in a hot oven for twenty minutes until the rice has absorbed all the stock. This makes a delicious "bed" for creamed chicken or shrimps à la Newburg. Or even for poached eggs.

Have you ever extemporized a dessert by grilling bananas for fifteen minutes (in their skins) and then serving sugar and cinnamon with them?

Have you ever ripped open a package of English muffins, toasted these, broiled thin slices of ham (from a tin), poached eggs and called on a jar of ready-made hollandaise sauce to turn out a dish of eggs Benedict at literally five minutes' notice?

Or used the muffins to carry slices of ham and grilled mushrooms?

Or slices of sausage meat, fried and topped with a rich mushroom sauce? (You can use a can of mushroom soup as a base for this and add fresh mushrooms, seasonings and sherry.)

Here is a list of emergency rations to go on a special party shelf in your pantry:

Canned soups of various kinds.

Canned clam chowder. (If you don't know it already try the New England type of clam chowder put up by Davis and Co., Glouces-ter, Mass. Try some of their other fish specialties too. I can recommend their canned shad roe.)

Canned turtle soup with sherry.

Clam juice cocktail.

Canned tomato juice for cocktails and to make tomato aspic for salads and for sauces and casserole dishes.

Maggi bouillon cubes.

Hams, boned and put up in tins.

Canned baked beans.

Canned julienne potatoes.

Canned fried-onion rings.

Pumpernickel, in a tin (35¢).

Plain biscuits in tins.

Devonshire Melba toast.

Baba au Rhum (one cake, weight 1½ lbs., $1.50).

Crepes suzettes (9-oz. jar holds 14, costs $2.00).

Wild strawberry preserves (for breakfast, tea or as a dessert with cream cheese or cottage cheese).

Syrian honey (in a really lovely colored pottery jar).

Bar le Duc (to be eaten with game or as a dessert with cream or cottage cheese).

Major Grey's India Chutney (if you can still get it).

Pickled walnuts (delicious with cold roast beef).

Tarragon vinegar.

Worcestershire sauce.

A.I. sauce.

Kitchen bouquet.

Herbs for seasoning. (Why not get one of the collections put up six jars to a box for $2.00?)

Olives.

Anchovy paste. (Use on biscuits or Melba toast for canapés, on toast under poached or scrambled eggs, or to make *beurre anchois* for fish.)

½ lb. Parmesan cheese to be grated as needed.

Noodles and Italian spaghetti.

Artichoke hearts (for salads or to be cut and tossed into an omelet).

Merritt's Beaten Biscuits (one dozen in a package, 25¢).

Tea (Earl Grey's Mixture) or some other very, very good variety. Keep it in a caddy and use it by spoonfuls. Abolish the muslin teaball and discover what really fine tea tastes like.

Sherry, rum, domestic brandy for cooking and domestic wines in half-gallon demijohns.

Champagne.

## Week-End Appetites

IN ADDITION to all the things you order for the meals you have planned for week-end entertaining, it's a safe precaution to add a few extras that you can fill in with if extra guests turn up or if you and your friends get too terribly hungry after swimming or playing games.

You'll face those increased appetites with an easy mind if you know your refrigerator holds:

Several extra cans of soup chilling into jelly.

A package or two of frozen vegetables (peas, lima beans, cut fresh corn, broccoli).

A package or two of frozen raspberries or sliced peaches.

Lay in some English muffins for emergency rations. And brush up your skill in making baking-powder biscuits. You can run up a panful of these while your guests are drinking their first round of cocktails. Serve them piping hot with butter and honey or strawberry jam. Or make them a little larger and use them for shortcakes, with raspberries, strawberries or peaches and lots of extra-rich cream. Or with vanilla ice cream which you have telephoned for to the drugstore.

Above all, learn to make perfect coffee. Choose any method you like (delicious coffee can be made by any way ever devised). You can use a percolator or a Silex or a drip pot or an old-fashioned pot in which the coffee is boiled with egg and a pinch of salt. But make it strong, and make it uniformly good.

A lot of worse things can be said of a woman than "she gives you a good cup of coffee."

# 14

## MAKE THEM WANT TO COME BACK

### The Secret of Success

Just giving your guests a gay and entertaining evening with games they enjoy playing, plenty of delicious food, laughter and fun isn't enough to make them count the days until you ask them again.

People nowadays aren't so hard up for fun as all that. They enjoy it, of course, as who doesn't? But still they look for something more. Just having the reputation (justly earned) of being a clever and amusing hostess won't win you a wide and enthusiastic circle of friends who would rather come to your house—even for cheese, beer, doughnuts and coffee—than go to an elaborate party anywhere else in town.

When a party is over what lingers in the minds of everyone who was there isn't only the gaiety or the stunts, the colorful decorations, the delicious food, the music or what people were wearing. People carry away with them from a party the feeling of enjoyment, and what they keep on remembering is the *feeling that they were wanted*. The feeling that it really mattered to the host and hostess that they were there and enjoyed themselves. The feeling that their hosts are genuinely interested in them and *care for them individually*.

If you can give your guests this feeling when you ask them to your house then they will surely want to come back.

## How It's Done

No WAY has ever been devised of counterfeiting an interest in others. *It has to be real* to work at all. You can be punctilious about all the etiquette of entertaining, but if this doesn't spring from a genuine and heartfelt liking for others you won't convince anyone that your good manners are anything more than a manner. People will shy away from you instead of being drawn to you. They may not know what it is that makes them hold off. They may tell each other that Mrs J—— is always so sweet and kind to everyone and isn't it extraordinary how she never seems to forget anyone's birthday? But the house they like best to go to and want to be asked to again and again won't be *yours*.

If what you really want in life is to be really successful and popular as a hostess *you must start by liking people*. You must find them (even the ones who have the unhappy reputation of being bores) interesting.

## Bores—and How to Bear Them

REFORM THEM. Yes, I mean just that.

Turn them from bores into human beings. Of course you may not be able to transform Miss C—— who has two topics of conversation—her last operation and her next one—into a scintillating or amusing dinner partner. But you can, with a little adroit maneuvering, steer Miss C—— away from the operating room into the allied topic of hospital management and thence into the modern question of socialized medicine. Presently Miss C—— may find to her surprise that she is contributing to a really exciting general discussion. Perhaps she has always known deep down in her heart that people considered her rather dull, "almost a bore." Yet here she is, shining. She'll be grateful to you all the rest of her days. And you will have had the fun of giving everybody (including Miss C——) a surprise.

Often what passes for boredom is shyness. A person who feels at a loss can't think of anything interesting to talk about. It may be a feeling of inferiority or of not being wanted.

Give the shy man something to do which will help to make the party go and watch his shyness disappear. Ask him to mix some special drink you may happen to know he makes well and likes to make. Ask him to tend the bar. Or to be captain of one side in a game.

Flatter the woman who insists on talking about *her* children, *her* house and herself by asking her advice on some question that concerns yours. This will have the effect of startling her out of her old boring pattern into being a real human being. And what she says may be quite worth while and give you a few pointers too.

Nearly everyone has at least *one* enthusiasm. If you can find out what this is and talk to that person about it you will discover a point of interest. If *your* mind is really open and alive it can find anything from Mayflower ancestry to Siamese cats' food for an hour's conversation.

## We All Want to Be Liked

PEOPLE ARE ALWAYS FLATTERED by a hostess who remembers their little personal preferences—that Mr A—— has a weakness for three lumps of sugar in after-dinner coffee, that Miss B—— never eats tomatoes in any form, that Mrs C—— prefers a clam-juice cocktail to one made of alcohol before dinner.

These things aren't hard to remember if you train your mind to record them. If your mind just won't at first then keep a little notebook and jot down little points about your friends and the people you meet and go over the pages from time to time until your memory gets on the job.

If you entertain a great deal, perhaps at buffet meals, don't get in the way of always having the same menu. People don't want to know when they are asked to your house that there will inevitably be chicken à la crème. You can keep a record of your parties and the guests at them and what you gave the guests to eat, and then you won't confront Mr J—— with the same dish for the seventh time you have invited him to dinner.

If you have a special dish, one which is particularly yours and which you make extremely well, then feature that by all means. Especially if it is something you know your friends do not have at their own homes or get anywhere else. And if they have given you actual evidence that they like it by eating quantities of it at some time.

Don't jump to the conclusion that they like it because *you do*, like the hostess who always serves a casserole of Italian spaghetti which is so heavy with garlic that her friends avoid it. "It's such a good dish," she laments, "but nobody seems to eat it."

If Mrs G—— has praised your corn muffins send her the recipe for them. And ask her to tea some afternoon and have a batch of corn muffins especially for her. She might like half a dozen to take home with her to share with Mr G——

People like to feel that your interest in them lasts beyond the hours when they are in your house or arriving on your doorstep. It means a lot to them to know that you think of them at other times, that when you are on a motor trip in New England you remember how proud Miss B—— is that she had a Massachusetts great-grandmother and send her a picture postcard from Salem or Newburyport. A letter written to someone while you are off on a delightful trip can mean a great deal. For one thing, if you are having a wonderful time the letter will have a lot of vitality in it. And if it's not about what *you* are doing and seeing and having, but about some sight or little experience which you know the person to whom you write would be interested in, then such a letter is really a gift. One of the nicest presents anyone can receive.

A young girl who went to Ireland for a summer's holiday had very little money to spend on gifts for her friends who had seen her off gaily. Instead she bought a big basket of Irish peat and sent a block of it, wrapped up in green-and-white paper, to each of her friends for their Christmas fires.

Cultivate the habit and the art of writing really warm and charming little notes. It's quite customary to write letters to people who have lost some member of the family and, of course, to write to one's hostess after a week-end visit. But a few words of appreciation to someone who has done some little thing for you, or who, you happen to know, has just had a stroke of good fortune, who has been invited to go off on a cruise, or is planning to build a new house, will give that person an amount of pleasure out of all proportion to the size of the note or the amount of time it takes to write it. I can still remember the notes from people who wrote me when I left my house and of the good times they had had there.

Most of all, people like to see their friends alone sometimes. Read again what we said in Chapter Four about this. They never are really sure that you like them unless you show that you enjoy having them sometimes with no other guests. Even at quite a big party you can find time to talk for a few moments at least with each one of your guests, making them feel that you like them *for themselves.*

## The Spirit of Welcome

SEVERAL YEARS ago an old lady whom I knew was wakened in the night by a sound she knew must be a burglar in the dining room. She was almost ninety years old but she was not in the least afraid. She got into a warm dressing gown and slippers and padded downstairs to be in time to save her silver tea set if possible.

There *was* a burglar, though fortunately not a very ferocious one. He seemed almost more frightened of Mrs Warren than she was of him. So much so that she set about scolding him for breaking in her house, "and on Christmas Eve too." The burglar muttered that he didn't know about Christmas. This shocked Mrs Warren even more. She ordered him to sit right down at once and she sat down and proceeded to tell him all about Christmas. I don't know but what she finished by making him a cup of hot cocoa and giving him five dollars to buy his family a Christmas dinner.

I heard this story and not long afterward I saw Mrs Warren. I told her how perfectly wonderful I thought she was. Her reply was that when she found the noise really *was* a burglar she thought at once of a story she had heard about her great-grandmother who lived in Tennessee in the days when the Cherokees were to be dreaded. She was just a girl and very beautiful (the great-grandmother when she was married and went out to Tennessee to live in the great house her husband had built for her. Not long afterward her husband had to be away from home for some time, and during those days the word went round that the Indians were preparing to raid the settlement. The young bride was advised to run away with some of the neighbors. But she refused to do this and leave her husband's property to the Indian raiders. Instead she stationed a servant to keep watch and then told the others to cook all the food in the house for a feast. She had a long table set in the hall of the house, put out her silver and tall candlesticks, as for a party. Then she went upstairs and dressed herself in her white satin wedding dress with the long lace veil. When the sentinel called that the Cherokees were coming across the fields the bride went downstairs, threw open the door and, carrying a bowl full of rice, met the first of the savages at the open front door. She held out the rice in welcome.

It was a gesture even the Cherokees could not misunderstand. They must have been startled by this lovely young girl in her billowing white satin and floating veil, but they knew the symbolism of rice, and they could see, over their hostess's shoulder, the waiting dining table and all the good food prepared for them.

They came in and ate the dinner and left everything else on the plantation untouched. And from that day onward that house, that land and the members of that family were as safe with the Indians as members of the Cherokee tribe.

## Clever, but Not Too Clever

No ONE WANTS TO SIT in the audience *all* the time. Can you let someone else take a trick in the conversation once in a while? Can you leave someone else's story uncapped (difficult though this is) even though you may have a better one at the tip of your tongue? Can you listen? Not as if you were doing it under pressure while your mind ran off somewhere else, but as though you were as much interested in hearing what someone else has to say as you are in having them listen to you?

Maybe you do happen to know more about Early American glass or politics or the temperaments of Sealyhams than the person does who is talking about these things. Do you have to correct them as they go along and finally brush them to one side while *you* take the floor?

Can you lose an argument when it may mean making a friend? Or keeping one?

Are you tolerant of others' mistakes? A woman whose life had given her a much wider knowledge of the world than the people had with whom she had to live for some time was shocked to find herself correcting her friends as they talked. True, some of their statements weren't correct. But what if they weren't? Suppose one of them was a bit vague about the location of Kansas City; it wasn't a matter of buying a railroad ticket to a wrong destination. This woman tells me she started a game with herself. She lets three errors go by, unchecked, and only pounces on the fourth if it is one that really affects the argument. And she is finding life much pleasanter and herself more popular too.

If you are one of the people who do a lot of things outstandingly well can you keep from doing them occasionally in order to give others a chance to shine? Can you sit gracefully on the side lines and really enjoy another's playing? And without saying to yourself that of course you could do it a lot better?

Check yourself on these things. Very often the clever person is at a disadvantage. She's got to be cleverer than clever to *be*, and not just *have*, a success.

There are half a dozen women whose names history remembers as really perfect hostesses. All of them were clever women. They must have been so. But all of them established their immortal reputation by being able to make other people feel, and often be, clever. They had the gift for drawing others out, and they are remembered for that gift and not for what *they* said or did.

## Parties to Remember

EVERY PARTY, no matter how small or how simple, should have an element of beauty. Again I repeat, I don't mean necessarily elaborate. Certainly all of us should be under an obligation to create as much of beauty as possible in our lives. Doesn't this extend to the times when we ask our friends to be with us?

If you are so fortunate as to have a really beautiful or picturesque house or a charming garden or a terrace with a view you can find hundreds of ways of entertaining so as to give your friends the feeling that they have been asked to take part in something to be remembered.

Not long ago I heard about a French lady who had a magnificent house in the old part of Paris. In the rear was a grand formal garden with high green hedges and, on each side, planked with colonnades.

She and her husband were both talented amateur actors and they conceived the delightful idea of giving a Venetian party in which they themselves and a few selected friends would enact *The Merchant of Venice*. I was not there myself, but I was told it was beautiful beyond words. Everyone came in Venetian costume of the period. The gardens were softly lit with indirect lighting, and the guests sat around informally while the actual play took place. Surely a party like this which remains in the memory of all those who were there was worth the money and effort expended on it.

I remember a ball I went to in Newport a number of years ago. The house stood on a high rocky point, jutting into the harbor, and on one side, a little sand cove. It was, of course, an evening party and the gardens were floodlighted. There was dancing on a floor that had been laid under the trees. Down along the cove a gypsy encampment had been set up with tents and glowing campfires with big cauldrons hung over them—and there were gypsy fortunetellers too. Out in the harbor the square-rigged yacht, the Aloha, rode at anchor, all hung with colored lights, and a little launch was waiting to carry the guests out whenever they wished to go.

It's true very few people can summon gypsies and sailing yachts at a moment's notice when they give a party. But also, and this I think is really quite appalling, there are many people who really spend a great deal of money on entertaining without giving their friends anything distinctive or beautiful to remember.

It isn't as though they didn't want to. Or that they can't think of beautiful things to do. It's ever so much sadder than that . . . it's *laziness and fear which holds them back*, the silly fear of doing something which hasn't been done before. It just seems easier to ask people to play bridge or to play the games they are accustomed to playing.

But, on the other hand, there are people who accept this obligation to give others beauty when they can afford to do it. In this connection I think of a well-known Baltimore woman who has awakened a whole community to her own intense love of music. Every spring and every fall she engages a string quartet for a season of six weeks. Four or five times each week during these "seasons" her friends are invited to concerts of chamber music in the big music room she planned and decorated especially for this.

Here again is the giving of beauty to friends in a way which will long be remembered.

## Is It Worth Doing?

EACH ONE OF US must answer that for herself. You know what *you* think and, having read this book, you know what I think about it too.

Every single thing that makes your life fuller and richer is worth doing. Every person who widens your horizon is worth knowing. Friends aren't just people you can do things *for*. They are people who do things *for* you. My conviction is that

> *LOVE that fulfills you,*
> *FRIENDS who delight you,*
> *WORK that intrigues you,*
> *BEAUTY which enchants you,*

these are the rocks to build upon for health, success and joy.

These are the secret keys to making living fun.

Dorothy Draper
The Hampshire House
150 Central Park South
New York, N. Y.

# BIBLIOGRAPHY

*Etiquette*, Emily Post. Funk and Wagnalls.

This is the one, comprehensive, really authoritative book on the subject, written by someone who really knows. If you expect to entertain an ambassador, an archbishop or an aviator's fiancée, Mrs Post will tell you all you want to know about how to do this graciously and charmingly.

*Decorating Is Fun!*, Dorothy Draper. Doubleday, Doran & Co., Inc.

If you have liked ENTERTAINING IS FUN! and if you have found it stimulating and helpful, we think you'll find DECORATING IS FUN! equally worth while. It tells you what you can do to your house and to your furniture to make them interesting and lovely to live with. And how to have the kind of house you've often dreamed of having "some day."

*Constance Spry's Garden Note Book*. Alfred A. Knopf.

Full of garden lore and ideas for flower arrangement. Written by a real gardener who manages to bring her magic indoors.

*The Boston Cooking School Cook-Book*, by Fannie Farmer. Little, Brown & Co.

The most practical, generally useful cook book we know. With this book in one hand and a well stocked pantry you can face any domestic crisis which involves feeding people with perfect equanimity.

*America's Cook Book*, compiled by the Herald Tribune Home Institute. Charles Scribner's Sons.

A thick volume of recipes drawn from all parts of the country and presenting an all-American array that can't be beaten for flavor and food values. Gives you the "American way" in cooking as American cooks have originated it.

*Elsie De Wolf's Recipes for Successful Dining*, Elsie de Wolf (Lady Mendl). Harper Bros.

Some of the dishes given in this book are pretty elaborate and call for practised chefs. Sometimes for a half-dozen of them. But if you want to learn how to make a dozen or so really superb dishes, sauces to make an epicure lift his eyebrows in ecstasy, we recommend that you study this. Not all the recipes are terrifying. For instance, you'll find that useful dodge with rice and canned soup we mentioned in Chapter Thirteen here. We recommend the soups, the sauces and above all the iced desserts. There's a recipe for pineapple ice that makes our mouth water even remembering it.

*June Platt's Party Cook Book*. Houghton Mifflin Company.

Mrs Platt is an expert cook and her recipes are the result of a real flair for food. By all means add this to your list of valuable cook books.

*Successful Kitchenette Cooking*, The Herald Tribune Home Institute.

What kind of menus and what recipes can be cooked successfully in a kitchenette. Also lists equipment that is really useful. If you cook for two you'll find this helpful.

*Successful Buffet Suppers*, The Herald Tribune Home Institute.

Menus, recipes and directions how to serve as many as twenty or thirty guests simply and without a fuss.

*Savory Sauces and Gravies*, The Herald Tribune Home Institute.

How to make these. Practical and explicit.

*Successful Cooking Primer*, The Herald Tribune Home Institute.

Ten lessons with menus and recipes for the new, inexperienced cook.

*Music for Everybody*, Sigmund Spaeth. *Leisure League Little Book No. 9.*

*The Week-End Book:* A Sociable Anthology edited by Frances and Vera Meynell. Random House.

Contains all the old-fashioned games that everyone remembers having played when they were children and no one remembers exactly *how* to play. Riddles, limericks, guessing games, charades, songs, recitations. Actually invaluable to have in the house when you have a week-end party and it looks like rain.

*The Life of the Party*, Fred Menaker and Franklin Folsom. *Leisure League Little Book No. 11.*

Games anyone can play anywhere and have fun.

# ACKNOWLEDGMENTS

THE DRAWINGS IN THIS BOOK have been prepared by Jay Warmuth. Credit is also given to Hans Van Nes for the photographs of Setting the Stage, Afternoon Tea at Home (this room was designed by David Adler, architect), Eight for Supper (the beautiful antique dinner plates are from William H. Plummer & Company, and the earthenware baking dishes are from Hammacher Schlemmer Co., Inc.); First Impressions and The Hostess's Treasure Chest (all the objects in this photograph are from Hammacher Schlemmer and Company, Inc.); to Emelie Danielson for the photograph The Meal Outdoors and to Nyholm for the photograph Counting the Inches.

# INDEX

237

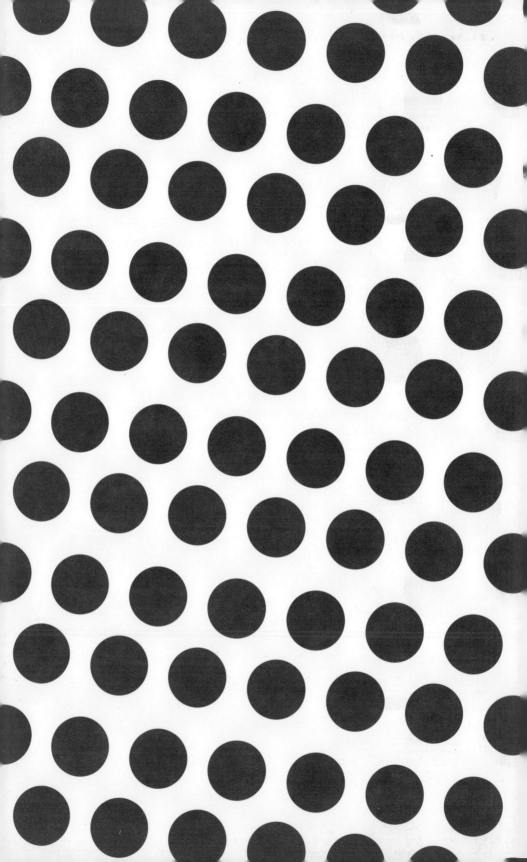